What other authors are saying about this book

"Readers may think the tragic women of Vancouver's Downtown Eastside were unloved, neglected and ignored. Meet Bonnie Fournier, not just "Mom" to so many of these women, but a gifted psychiatric nurse who took loving care of them as she patrolled the city's poorest postal code in her health van night after night, year after year. Cleaning their wounds was only part of her job; what was just as important was the friendship, practical advice and kindness she dispensed with the bandages and medicine.

Before she started working on the Health Van, Bonnie did the medical assessments of people who had just been arrested and put in cells in the Downtown Eastside's Main Street police station. Among them were Willie Pickton and his brother Dave, and even then she had a bad feeling about this pair. Bonnie is one of the Downtown Eastside's heroes and her story will inspire you … and break your heart."

Stevie Cameron, author of *On the Farm: Robert William Pickton and the Tragic Story of Vancouver's Missing Women*

Mugged, Drugged and Shrugged

The Wrong Side of the Eastside

Bonnie Fournier

with a foreword by Elaine Allan

Order this book online at www.trafford.com
or email orders@trafford.com

Most Trafford titles are also available at major online book retailers.

Editorial and production coordination by GF Murray Creative Information Solutions, Coquitlam, BC
Cover painting by Melissa Tulloch, Pender Harbour, BC
Author photo by Manny Cu

Canadian Cataloguing in Publication Data

Printed in the United States of America.

ISBN: 978-1-4251-2506-6 (sc)
ISBN: 978-1-4251-2507-3 (hc)
ISBN: 978-1-4251-2508-0 (e)

Library of Congress Control Number: 2010915621

*Our mission is to efficiently provide the world's finest, most comprehensive book publishing
service, enabling every author to experience success. To find out how to publish your book,
your way, and have it available worldwide, visit us online at www.trafford.com*

Trafford rev. 10/29/2010

 www.trafford.com

North America & international
toll-free: 1 888 232 4444 (USA & Canada)
phone: 250 383 6864 ♦ fax: 812 355 4082

Mugged, Drugged and Shrugged

The Wrong Side of the Eastside

Dedication

All that I am or ever hoped to be, I owe to an angel:
my mom, Phyllis Margery Horne, R.N. (1918–2003)

Acknowledgements and gratitude to:

My family and dear old Aunt Jess

My editor, Kedre Murray

Nancy Hawkins, who took many of the interior photos

The executive director of W.I.S.H., Kate Gibson

My friends Diane Ashworth, Raye Rowe, Charlotte and Hayden Hooley, Marion Parr, Sheila Leach, Wendy Pederson, Jean Swanson, Stevie Cameron and Elaine Allan.

Special mention and hugs to:

Manny Cu—I really miss you!

Melissa Tulloch for her original cover—such a talent!

The sheriffs who created such lasting memories for me, the Carnegie Centre, W.I.S.H. Society and the Vancouver street nurses.

I will never forget my guys, gals and family tragedies of the D.T.E.S.

God bless you all.

Contents

Part One: Mugged

Part Two: Drugged

Foreword
by Elaine Allan

I met Bonnie Fournier in 1998 while working at the W.I.S.H. Drop-In Centre on Vancouver's Downtown Eastside, in the country's poorest postal code, a block up from the notorious open drug market on the corner of Main and Hastings. The Drop-In Centre (inside the First United Church) provided dinner, respite from the street, hot showers and access to the D.E.Y.A.S. Health Van to the neighbourhood's sex trade workers.

Bonnie Fournier had her hands full when the D.E.Y.A.S. Health Van pulled up to the side doors at the W.I.S.H. Drop-In Centre each night at 6:30 PM. The women who needed her help would wait patiently to see her, knowing that they would never be turned away.

The Health Van had been customized with a special ceiling that provided headroom and shelving and doors that could hold medical supplies. Regardless of how long the line-up outside the Health Van could get, Bonnie made time to see each woman who needed to see her and she always knew how to make them feel special before the Van had to leave for another service location.

Once inside the D.E.Y.A.S. Health Van, the women of W.I.S.H. were treated to first-rate medical care. Most would simply feel better just being in the company of a warm and caring professional nurse.

Bonnie worked hard dispensing Tylenol, lozenges, multi-vitamins, laxatives and Epsom salts. She also gave flu vaccines, bandaged wounds and did her best to soothe battered women. Sometimes W.I.S.H patrons lined up just to talk to Bonnie and get one of her famous hugs. Bonnie had many nicknames but she was often called "Mom"—the highest compliment that could be paid to a woman by the sex trade workers at the Centre.

Bonnie knew many of the women who frequented the W.I.S.H. Drop-In Centre from her days working as the nurse inside the city cells. The city cells, or the "city bucket" as it was often referred to, were located underneath the courthouse at 222 Main Street on Vancouver's Downtown Eastside. Prisoners were kept in cells while they waited to be escorted upstairs by the sheriffs. Upstairs housed the courtroom where prisoners would make court appearances in front of various judges. The city bucket was known for being a cold, damp space with harsh lighting. Bonnie, from her years working with the city bucket population, had developed excellent diagnostic skills and was adept at identifying the illnesses that plagued the women of W.I.S.H.

Most of my clients battled serious addiction issues. Heroin and crack cocaine were the drugs of choice and many of the women I knew used both. Working in the sex trade and being a drug addict is a high-risk lifestyle. Women who worked the streets of Vancouver's Downtown Eastside contracted HIV, hepatitis C, S.T.Ds, endocarditis and lung infections at an alarming rate. They were also subjected to "bad dates," men who posed as customers but were really violent predators in disguise. It wasn't uncommon for the women Bonnie encountered outside the doors of the W.I.S.H.

Centre to be in need of some serious medical treatment for things like stab wounds and broken bones.

For fear of being disregarded as mere drug addicts, women who frequented the W.I.S.H. Drop-In Centre were often reluctant to seek health care from traditional service providers. Bonnie Fournier, or "Nurse Ratched," (another of Bonnie's many street monikers, based on the dictatorial nurse in the 1975 film *One Flew Over the Cuckoo's Nest*) did not fit into the street population's perception of a traditional health care provider. Bonnie had a fun, casual side that was underlined by a serious, calming nature. The women of the Downtown Eastside knew that Bonnie would take their concerns seriously and would do whatever she could do to help them. If Bonnie believed a woman to have an illness that required hospitalization, she would arrange for them to be transported to St. Paul's Hospital. Bonnie would then follow up on the women she referred to St. Paul's with phone calls to triage nurses, doctors and social workers. None of Bonnie's actions guaranteed that a woman from W.I.S.H. would receive the treatment she needed but it usually meant that she would not be turned away by hospital staff at the receiving doors. Any doctor who dismissed a referral from Bonnie Fournier and the D.E.Y.A.S. Health Van could find themselves in the undesirable position of talking to Bonnie Fournier about the Hippocratic Oath.

Sometimes I could make out Bonnie's strong, grey-haired, slender shape from a block or two in the distance while driving myself out of the Downtown Eastside after closing the centre at night. Bonnie always wore a bright blue Gore-tex jacket with NURSE written in reflective tape across the back. The Health Van, too, was blue with D.E.Y.A.S. written in reflective lettering across its sides.

Bonnie and I often talked about the women that we knew from the Downtown Eastside neighbourhood who were going missing. Women had started to disappear from the neighbourhood at a disturbing rate. Together we would talk to police officers, politicians, social workers, you name it, trying to raise awareness about some of the sex trade workers who were vanishing, seemingly without leaving a clue as to where we might find them.

I left the W.I.S.H. Drop-In Centre in 2001. A year later, in 2002, Robert Pickton was arrested and later charged with the murders of many of the neighbourhood's missing sex trade workers. While in police custody, Robert Pickton would admit to murdering forty-nine women. Bonnie and I have shared many laughs over the years, but sadly, we have shared many more tears. Bonnie was the last person to see Sereena Abotsway—a woman who accessed both the W.I.S.H. Drop-In Centre and the D.E.Y.A.S. Health Van, and one of the women Robert Pickton was convicted of killing. As the years rolled along and ensuing court proceedings revealed horrifying details of some of the murders of women we knew, Bonnie and I would cling to each other, fighting tears and promising ourselves that we would continue to work to create services and awareness for marginalized women.

Without question, Bonnie Fournier's work as a registered nurse touring the streets of Vancouver's Downtown Eastside in the D.E.Y.A.S. Health Van will not be forgotten in my lifetime. Throughout my life I will forever remember Bonnie and the D.E.Y.A.S. Health Van as a beacon of humanity that faithfully came at 6:30 each night, and parked in front of the doors of the W.I.S.H. Drop-In Centre.

Vancouver
July 14, 2010

Part One:
Mugged

Introduction

I am a retired registered psychiatric nurse, and I was employed on the streets in the downtown core of Vancouver, British Columbia. I have experiences to share: some scary, some shocking—and all too true.

I will show my respect for confidentiality by altering names in this book. The pictures here are a thousand words of true care, trust and a cup half-full. I am striving to fill that cup by advocating for treatment and recovery.

Some left their footprints on my legs, arms and back until I mastered ducking, dodging and darting. The most memorable footprints are on my heart, kept warm and never to be forgotten.

My purpose is to share my joys, smiles and tears covering twenty-eight years of forensic nursing in the provincial court holding cells and eight years of nursing on the streets of the Downtown Eastside. I want you to see pictures through my words and feel a part of the laughter, tears, joy and fears of a forgotten society. I want you to be educated, informed and to understand the realities of addiction, violence and devastation.

Most importantly, I want you to be aware that the problems that exist in this society are not Monday to Friday, 9 AM to 5 PM with weekends and stats off—the problems are 24–7. They exist in every city, town and country in the so-called civilized world. What Vancouver, B.C. experiences is a large drop in the smouldering bucket of despair.

I was there—I began working with addicts and drug abusers in 1967. I chose my career path, and dedication kept me on it. After I retired from the provincial court cells, my working hours on the street were 1:30 PM to 2:30 AM. I saw, I felt, I listened and I learned. I cared for those who were suffering because society denied or interfered in the fulfillment of life's basic, primary needs.

I am so grateful to have the gag removed from my mouth. I am now free to speak my mind, providing concrete information about funding misuse and abuse. I want taxpayers to hear truths that cannot be denied. It's absolutely astounding how many millions of tax dollars are misdirected or misused. We need aggressive action for education, treatment and protection of the vulnerable citizen—all of us.

But the journey's not all doom and gloom. Come with me on a ride through the underside of our affluent society, and see for yourself.

One:
222 "Maim" Street

My four-and-a-half year old daughter held my hand as we waited for the light to change. She looked up at me and said, "I can't go in there, Mommy."

I turned to see what she was gesturing at and replied, "No, you can't go in there." She responded with, "No, it say, NO 5."

I did not give her any other explanations—she did not need any—she would be five in two weeks. Amused by her announcement, I squeezed her hand and made a mental note to share it with her dad during our own time, doing up the supper dishes.

No. 5 is a popular strip club on the corner of Powell and Main Streets. In the '70s and early '80s, its name was No. 5 Orange and it was well known for its great hamburgers. At least, that's according to guys who went there on their lunch breaks. They say it to this very day.

The gals there exhibited their physical attributes, but gyrations and lap dancing were considered indecent acts. The girls just sort of stood there and let it all hang out, I guess.

It was June 1979, and the weather was warm with a light breeze from the harbour. The noon-hour traffic was heavy. Working people were enjoying the nice weather on their lunch breaks in stark contrast to the yelling, shoving disagreements between slovenly street people nearby, or the person burrowed inside a roll of blankets sleeping in a doorway. I expected a frightened reaction from my daughter but she did not even tighten her grip on my hand. Perhaps she likened it to sibling rivalry at home in the "wreck" room with her brother?

It didn't take more than a few seconds of waiting. I knew that this was the place for me. It was "an opportunity for specialty employment in a unique environment." I was going for an interview at the Vancouver Provincial Courthouse, 222 Main Street, as the Sheriff's Nurse in the holding cells.

I wasn't nervous about the interview. I had worked on the anti-social side of nursing for more than ten years. This was a step in a slightly different direction, a change from my previous two years on the receiving end of verbal nurse-bashing at the Lakeside Correctional Centre for Women.

My little girl waited for the fifteen seconds it took for me to get the position—a real boost to my ego to be hired so quickly!

I was on Cloud Nine driving home: no more working shifts, holidays or weekends. Wow, the respected position of being the only nurse employed by Sheriff Court Services in British Columbia, working from 8 AM to 4 PM, Monday to Friday!

Two:
Let the Games Begin

A h yes, July 3, 1979—my first day as Flo Nightingale in the cells of Vancouver Provincial Courthouse. I collected my keys from the commissionaire, who directed me to a locked door leading down, down and yet another down into the bowels of 222 Main Street.

Provincial courthouse, with "wagon bay" at left.

I learned, from a deputy sheriff also collecting his keys, that I had been the only applicant for the nurse position. He also mentioned that the last nurse had only lasted one pay period in the cells. My, what enlightening information! I became somewhat apprehensive of the day ahead.

For laypersons' understanding, picture the holding cells located in the lower left gut area, between the descending colon and where used food exits the body. I also realized very quickly that this could be one small step for Bonnie the nurse and one giant step to avoid the potholes (or a-holes) in my way—not necessarily in that order.

The feeling of being the only leaf left on the branch ran through my mind that first day. I waited while the sheriffs searched prisoners from the city bucket and directed them to cell #5.

You can use your own definition of "city bucket," but whatever was in that bucket they brought it with them! A major task for nurses early in training is to develop sense awareness. The gift of smell is one sense to leave at home. It's also good to avoid taking any home at the end of a shift! I was a seasoned mouth-breathing nurse, but there was still the odd time when I swore I could actually taste it. The scent is identifiable, beyond expectations, if you nose breathe.

It became very clear from the get-go why Phew Do or the more potent Kennel #5 cologne should have been a mandatory sheriff uniform requirement. It occurred to me that a back-up intervention of Scotch Mints up the nostrils could satisfy Workers Comp coverage against inhaling any ambient toxic waste and subsequent upchucking. I made a mental point of recommending that both be standard issue on the uniform duty belt, in close proximity to the handcuffs.

A sheriff searching a prisoner instructed me to remain well back from the cell gate until all was secure. Four sheriffs searched more than thirty guys transported that morning from the overnight

Vancouver Police (V.P.D.) holding cells. The V.P.D. was called "312" for those in the know, but I was not yet an accepted member of the in-the-know team. I still had to pass cell #5 to face proper in-the-know testing by the staff and prisoners.

I received clearance, dusted cobwebs off my cap, adjusted my uniform, maintained a strong, professional attitude and strode briskly past cell #5. The cell looked like a tin of sardines—packed. The smell emanating from it also matched the sardines, with a dash of other gaseous emissions. It suited the title of "new fish" given to first-time remands by the frequent flyers.

Foot, crotch and armpit fragrances greeted me. Most days the cells were crowded with prisoners who hadn't accessed soap and water in a day or two. Some occupants were vulnerable due to mental health issues, going through life with their horn stuck— victims themselves who fell through the many cracks in our justice system. On this day, those charged had spent a holiday weekend in the V.P.D. lock-up. Comments by the sheriffs doing the search, and by the other prisoners, were as colourful as the smell. (Some guests to our cells required separate housing, hosing down and a complete change of clothing courtesy of the Sally Ann boutique, God bless them!)

Not surprisingly, I observed that the sheriffs' hand-washing technique, with green soap or Hibitane cleanser, was comparable to a surgeon's pre-op routine—no workshop would be required by yours truly.

My first day on the job just happened to follow a three-day weekend. It had the added bonus of being two days before the welfare cheques arrived. Whoopee, more than 200 smelly inmates with attitude problems, waiting up to six hours for their court appearances. They usually stayed for more than eight hours, until the court appearance decision documents for prisoner release or remand in custody were available for the Sheriff Records Officer to process.

The air was always bad in the holding areas anyway—with or without prisoners. The low ceilings, concrete floors and walls, old plumbing and steel bars and benches did not react favourably to the strong germicidal solution used daily by maintenance staff.

I know that I have previously referred to nurses as mouth-breathers, but I simply could not pass by cell #5 with my mouth open. A professional air of confidence emanated from my person as I walked past and into the holding cell control office in stalwart fashion, holding my breath all the way. I do not recommend holding your breath for quite as long as I did that morning. Blue lips can be a dead giveaway.

I was acutely aware that the six sheriffs, all male, were checking out my attitude, and perhaps my attributes. I have never had much in the way of physical attributes; it was warm down there and any visual up-and-down of my body would confirm the lack. Hell, even on a cold day I was pointless!

The first sheriff to speak to me was the Sheriff III, who was in charge of the court holding cells. He introduced me to the rest of the sheriffs as "the new nurse."

I had an inkling that the lads were individually determining whether I would cry, last longer than the previous nurse or take it on the chin. Little did they know that this nurse had arrived with a ton of psychiatric nursing experience. I could take it, I could dish it out—no Betsy Bedpan here! I loved all challenging experiences—mental, physical and emotional.

Nurse Ratched had landed, so let the games begin. Go ahead and make my day.

And make it they did—the fifth-floor supervisor phoned me not long later regarding a man "sleeping" on the lobby couch. I attended and found the fellow had suffered an overdose. We moved him to the floor and I commenced mouth-to-mouth assisted breathing while a sheriff monitored his pulse. The fellow did come out of it, but coughed in my mouth as he did.

I used a sheriff's toothbrush to brush my teeth afterwards with straight hydrogen peroxide. Where did I find the toothbrush? Well, the sheriff in question was known to be concerned about his oral care and had actually been observed to floss regularly. Strangely enough, oxygen tanks and mouth protectors appeared on every floor within a very short time, along with a stock of toothbrushes!

Three:
Bonnie and da Boyz

I learned a great deal from prisoners and sheriffs. I was the only female in the holding cells. The sheriffs referred to me as Bonnie the nurse because Bonnie the sheriff and Bonnie the payroll clerk were also on courthouse staff. Clarifying which Bonnie was required for what, who and where was a daily phone or paging necessity, because these other ladies did not show any interest in my daily duties.

It didn't take many shifts for me to get out of my nurse's starched whites and into a pantsuit. Forget the cap. It was lopsided most of the time anyway. I did keep my Clinics, though. They were duty shoes for the trenches, and there were many trench days to navigate.

I made a poor choice of uniform once and only once. It included white culottes (a skirt-shorts combination). A half-hour after I arrived at work, every sheriff in the holding cells was walking around with his pants rolled up to the knees!

Of course, it wasn't only me the sheriffs tried on. A sheriff showed up for work one day with a bandaid on his chin from shaving. You likely guessed it: within minutes every sheriff in the cells had a bandaid on his chin!

Somehow given the attitude of the sheriffs and prisoners the term "Head Nurse" wasn't quite appropriate for forensic nursing. I just changed my title to Nurse Supervisor when I was shown the full picture. It became very clear in short order that, as the lone female in the male holding cells, I was the sole target for comments. The prisoners in the cells often asked me to show my tits. Another favourite was, "Quit your grinnin' and drop your linen."

The inmates often sprawled on the floor or benches and talked to the ceiling. It was difficult to determine who was making the requests. Who cared? Not me! But the sheriffs were gentlemen in my presence. They cared, and informed the prisoners of the consequences if the comments continued. A particularly effective one was to tell the inmates the cell would be designated as non-smoking if the comments continued. It takes peer pressure (and a few band-aids) to heal sometimes!

I am a psychiatric nurse. I have the skills to address offensive issues of a personal nature in a mature, professional manner. During one of my "bad hair days" I would be prone to responding to such comments with, "I sense you have been incarcerated a long time!" This got me laughter and a positive response. My response toward the end of my service would have been, "You've been at sea a long time, sailor." Experience is the best teacher. I learned very quickly—it only took me twenty-eight years.

Professionals need to use an authoritative manner to appropriately manage prisoner behaviour. This is not meant as a rude or insulting statement to degrade the prisoner. Authoritative words of direction and clarification promote security and safety for all people involved.

Our Scots, Polish and other accented deputies entertained us with various verbal interpretations. One provided much laughter in the holding cells records office. A well-liked Polish escort deputy came into the records office and told the #1 Records Sheriff that he had to get a load of prisoners moved but one prisoner was not in Cell #5. He told us that he'd called the name about six times and nobody came forward. "Where is he?"

The senior records officer asked, "What is his name?" The sheriff replied, "Huggies," to which Records replied, "Hughes, Mark, not Huggies."

A Scottish sheriff, who reacted to the inmates' rude requests in his own professional, authoritative manner, used to say, "Shut yer gob, ya skunnert!" I had no idea what the phrase meant at the time, but the tone came through loud and clear. The order was all that was required as an effective form of behaviour modification.

I often directed the same phrase to that Scottish sheriff over the years. He used to greet me with, "Good morning, fair midden!" My retort was, "Shut yer gob, ya skunnert!" I was a great fan of Catherine Cookson novels so I knew the definition of midden—a Scottish term for a slop bin. We shared good laughs over Scottish colloquialisms over the years.

"Giving the nurse the gears" proved to be a daily amusement for the jail sheriffs. Nothing nasty, mind you, just cheeky. One sheriff, a former army sergeant, used to address me with, "Come here, Nurse, and let me snap your garters!" Often these boys of mine were a pain in close proximity to the appendix. I knew so many of them as baby deputies right on up to becoming supervisors, husbands and daddies. They loved to play jokes on me but I took it and I dished it out.

The sheriffs were not always very accepting of relief nurses. I had a helluva time arranging my vacation coverage, and forget sick days. I came to work, barfed, did my job and went home. Finally I was "paper trained" so that I only got sick on my days off.

All I had to do was mention that a nurse was coming into the holding area for orientation and the deputies would start whining.

"We don't want a Rent-a-Nurse; you don't need holidays; we don't like strange nurses; you are the only strange nurse that fits in down here..."

Most nurses were turned off just by coming into the holding cells. It was a dismal, dank, dark, dingy dungeon filled with dour-faced deputies—holding "score" numbers up for me to see behind their backs! I never saw a number indicating approval but none were ever seen by the visiting nurses, thank goodness. The same group of sheriffs always seemed to be involved in the snivelling, too. It was a group that liked to laugh but the jokes were quite innocent and tolerable.

I used to give them a lecture before a nurse covered her first shift in my absence. Think of the usual warnings that any mom would give her sons prior to the sitter's arrival: be good, be nice and just behave yourselves.

Usually I learned of a few incidents from the relief nurse on my return to work. In one case I got a message from the nurse that the shift was okay but the stethoscope was broken, and that she'd made note on the transfer medicals that BP checks had not been done. I examined the stethoscope and sure enough, I could hear nothing. How could there be, when the diaphragm end had been opened and stuffed with Kleenex?

In my absence, the relief nurse was often bombarded with requests for things that "Bonnie always does..." like bring the newspaper in, make copies of the crossword puzzle, buy lottery tickets for the jail staff, and other important nursing duties.

I told the relief nurse, "Always leave the cells for lunch and coffee breaks." I seldom did this myself, but I hoped she might do some more shifts when needed. If she didn't get out of there for a break from staff as well as prisoners, she would never last.

I always suggested that the relief nurse do an oxygen tank volume check on arrival in the cells. Oxygen on "flood" (setting 10) is quite effective in aiding recovery the morning after the night before. I didn't refuse the O_2 intervention but I insisted they allow me to administer it, and log the level left in the tank! The self medicating ceased pretty fast when I suggested to the staff that there would be a post-party sheriff assignment that would involve mouth-to-mouth breathing assistance for a prisoner if and when required.

The longest a relief nurse lasted was about a year. He was a nurse but was also completing his training as a naturopathic physician. The sheriffs found John quite entertaining and John was enthusiastic about sharing his expertise in recovery and healing through herbal, naturally prepared medicines.

He had many occasions to feel challenged in his approach. A few of the sheriffs enjoyed a party, so Monday mornings could be nasty after a weekend of various celebrations. One particularly popular intervention was John's liquid compound known as "Revival Drops." Three drops under the tongue apparently worked wonders, releasing extra enzymes into the system, which helped ease any discomfort.

I had an appointment one day so John worked the first half of my shift. I came into the records office to pick up the new remand names on my return to work. The records sheriff was at her desk and the assistant officer was at his desk directly facing her.

When I came into the office the assistant records officer told me that he was having a problem. His face was flushed and he appeared uncomfortable. I asked if he had eaten anything different that could have caused a reaction. The records sheriff said that John had given him three Revival drops under his tongue. I asked the young fellow what he was feeling like but he was very hesitant to tell me his symptoms. All he would say was that he couldn't stand up and had been feeling "unusual" for about a half-hour.

He eventually told me that he had *phallus erectus* (my definition, not his). He was quite anxious about it. It was very difficult not to laugh, but I proceeded to get him to drink volumes of water, plus some Maalox and a few Jolly Ranchers from my stock medications. The problem was rectified, or I guess you could say, de-rectified in a short time without any further intervention. John's drops certainly did create a revival in this case but not quite as intended. We laughed a lot about it afterward but it was initially only funny to the records sheriff and me, not to the patient at all.

This same sheriff told me he had a "gut ache" one day and asked if he could have some antacid. I told him, "Of course," so he went into the med drawer to take a med cup full. He returned to the records office and said, "When did they change the Maalox? It tastes like shit." I told him that the colour was white, as always, and the flavour was no different. He insisted, so I went with him to the drawer—only to find out that he had grabbed the bottle of calamine lotion and drunk an ounce! I verbally slapped him around a bit, then had him drinking copious amounts of water.

Just to be on the safe side, I phoned Poison Control to learn about any possible ill effects from ingesting calamine lotion. The first question I was asked was, "How old is the child?" I replied, "Oh, about twenty-eight..." No ill effects in the end, just some good laughs—medicine for all.

Don't take my comments as painting the sheriffs as an entirely rabble rousing group; it wasn't. Quite a few young single guys enjoyed playing pool, darts and socializing at the P.A.C. (Police

Athletic Club). It was a good place to wind down after a busy week. There were a few "I've fallen and can't reach my beer" instances.

I played Mom to these naughty boys and told them that if they partied hard at the P.A.C., please don't drive. Some people are inclined to feel invincible after a few jugs of suds. The P.A.C. was only a block away from the courthouse so I suggested that they walk over. They could have the commissionaire on duty let them in afterward and they could sleep on the cot in my office. Of course one clown had to comment, "Walk! You don't expect me to walk in that condition!"

When I arrived at work one morning, two sheriffs were squashed onto the narrow cot, head to foot. They'd wisely elected not to drive. A few aches from the army cot to go along with the aches in their heads proved experience to be the best teacher.

This last statement proved its effectiveness for me on one particular day. I received a call that a medical history was required on a very inebriated female. I was warned that she was verbally abusive, threatening and had to be kept separate because she wanted to fight everyone. When I arrived at the unit the female sheriff told me that this was not going to be an easy task.

A drunk usually communicates well with another drunk so I decided to interview this lady in the role of a drunk nurse. I went with the sheriff to talk to the woman a bit through the cell bars. The woman began yelling at first but I opened up my conversation with her with a slurred voice and a giggle and we bonded. In a matter of moments, she and I and the sheriff were moseying on down to the interview room.

I must tell you that I had warned the sheriff that I would be applying a different approach but she was not really sure what my plan entailed. The sheriff stood in her position outside the door, which was left ajar. I cannot describe her efforts at trying not to laugh. There was the odd point when I made eye contact with her to allow her to go elsewhere so she could let it all out of her system. I have the ability to keep a straight face, making it even harder for a third party to contain the humour.

It worked, though. "Iris" and I were best buds by the end of the head-to-toe assessment and had a few jokes and laughs interspersed here and there. We were just two happy drunks chatting about alcohol, drug abuse and withdrawal history. I took her blood pressure and showed her how to check mine. I had my arm around her shoulder and she had hers around mine as we went back to her cell.

It was an assessment moment that required a paradoxical approach and a really fun experience that the sheriff and I have never forgotten. I believe the sheriff was standing with her legs crossed at one point, if you get my drift!

This same sheriff, who became a dear friend over the years, was a person who could wrap the "baby sheriffs" (as she referred to the new ones) around her little finger. She was jovial and loved to laugh, and baked the most delicious muffins and loaves, bringing the goodies to work for everyone to enjoy. As you might expect, she was a very popular orientation leader for the "baby sheriffs."

This same sheriff also kept me up on my first aid intervention skills for staff. I swear that barely a week went by when she didn't fall, trip or slip on something while she was on her lunch break! It was not uncommon for her to come back with scrapes, and runs in her stockings. I told her that it was getting to the point where I was going to alert the ambulance service (E.H.S.) that my "Hopalong Casualty" sheriff buddy was on her break, so please tailgate her just in case.

I must stress there was no harm or malice intent toward me or anyone else, just mischief—spontaneously lightening the anxiety of the dank density of a worksite located a couple of hundred feet under the earth's surface, windowless and with five floors on top of us.

There was often laughter and good humour among the staff. Some inmates shared in the laughter as well. Some were so well-known that they were like family to the staff—it was akin to a family reunion in our cells when they came back in. One spring Thursday the elevator door opened to reveal one of the sheriffs dressed as the Easter Bunny and carrying a basket full of candy eggs. He hopped down the hall passing out eggs to all and sundry. All our "regulars" joined in the merriment... and enjoyed the candy.

Laughter brightened our darkest days. A fine line exists between laughter and tears. The laughter sure helped offset the tears and allowed us an outlet not directed at the prisoners. The choice was ours. I personally postponed tears for private times.

Four:
The Sheriffs

The cells seemed to be a punishment posting for sheriffs in the '70s and '80s. They may have shit-disturbed in another area, resulting in an involuntary transfer by management. Perhaps they forgot their neckties when the fall season arrived or wore a long-sleeved shirt in the summer season. The sheriff in command was a busy man in the olden days, sorting out that kind of naughty infraction. But I know, after my years there, that the sheriffs in the cells were the most competent, good-natured, professional and quick to respond of all.

I couldn't have cared less if the jail supervisor stapled up the hems on his uniform pants. There were so many scraps with prisoners some days that uniform pockets were routinely torn off or shirts ripped. I was too busy looking for blood and who it was coming from to worry about a uniform *faux pas*.

The team communicated instinctively, with few words required. Gut feelings played an important role in situational assessment. Everyone had an acute awareness of safety because of the constant potential for violence. For instance, we seldom knew what happened in court before prisoners returned to the cells. Some came through the door like a charging bull, screaming and fighting with no holds barred, no matter what.

Still, I was never given any reason to feel insecure, frightened or threatened by any prisoner. I knew my own vulnerable position. I also recognized that I could be a hazard in maintaining jail security. I required permission from the sheriff responsible for entry and exit to leave the control area before I moved past occupied cells, and I was informed when the stairs and elevator were secured for my use.

Sheriff deputies escorted me everywhere in the holding areas except the "sandbox." A sheriff was with me for all prisoner medical emergencies, and health assessment and transfer interviews. Many times two sheriffs were present based on the nature of the charges involved, experiences during the individuals' court appearances or a past history of unpredictable violence. I was always aware that I could be a potential hostage target. I was acutely aware of a security management problem if I did not follow the sheriffs' instructions. Safety was always paramount—for prisoners and staff. It was not a place for either the invincible or vulnerable personality.

The camaraderie did not seem as strong with other areas of the courthouse. Perhaps it was because they saw daylight more often! The rest of us endured seasonal times of darkness coming to work and darkness going home.

I recall an incident that showed how often the jail staffers were forgotten. One afternoon I came up from the cells to get some coffee, only to discover that the main floor and cafeteria were deserted.

I looked out the glass doors and saw pretty well every staff member (over three hundred of them!) standing on the other side of Main Street looking at me looking at them. When I opened the door to ask what was going on, they told me there had been a bomb scare. The building had been evacuated but no instruction or information was ever passed on to the jail "moles." Nobody even thought to tell us because, of course, we were safe—there were five floors of cindercrete block above us. Ya think?

Nobody had a longer posting down there than I did. I shit-disturbed a few times myself over the years and that occasion was one of them. I might add that when I did, it usually would be about staff and prisoner safety issues. Management and I had the occasional confrontation; some were humorous in retrospect, and some were serious. There was a pecking order in place. It depended on who the pecker was requesting or addressing the order.

In Sheriff Services, there is really only *one* sheriff. He or she is the highest level of appointed official and is in charge of Sheriff Court Services in a particular jurisdiction. All the others are actually Deputy Sheriffs I, II, III and so on, up to V status. The term "sheriff" is used here as a shortened verbal title. Can you imagine having to say, "I'm Deputy Sheriff I Smith and I am going to search you," sixty times a day? No con is interested in the whys, whats and wherefores anyway. In the cons' eyes you are a turnkey, a boss, a screw or other descriptor. Any longwinded title introduced before a search would likely get the following response from the prisoner involved: "I don't give a fuck who you are. Just don't squeeze my balls while you're doing it!"

I understand that the lengthy titles have recently been changed to Deputy Sheriff, Supervisor, Sergeant, Inspector, etc.—high time!

The sheriff is the person who oversees the fluid operation of all of Sheriff Services in a particular jurisdiction. He or she stays on top of problems or staffing issues through direct daily communication with deputy sheriffs in supervisory positions for the holding cells, courts and escort services.

The punishment label applied to cell postings for sheriffs changed significantly over the years. Sheriffs working in other areas eventually recognized the strength and cohesion of the teamwork in the holding cells and their interpretation of the job changed. I saw it evolve from my position on the outside looking in.

The deputy sheriff designated as the jail supervisor made a big difference in whether positive or negative feelings dominated among the staff. A competent supervisor earned respect. He made sure individual job performance was recognized and fostered an atmosphere of communication with an open-door policy. A good deputy sheriff supervisor also had the ability to discuss staff problems or issues with respect and confidentiality. Fairly regular jail staff meetings enabled everyone to have a voice.

Jail supervisors helped search, move prisoners and were in all ways a significant part of the team. They were not to be interpreted as peers but as an extra pair of hands. This made handling short-term staff shortages or managing fractious prisoners easier on the whole team. It also ensured that staffing or unsafe situations were visible so could be brought to the attention of management at their daily meetings.

Some sheriff supervisors over the years did not suit the jail position. I would be lying if I gave the idea that every one of them was hunky-dory. The atmosphere was fragile enough in the cells, and required a supervisor with an interest in communication and teamwork to gain the respect of the staff.

A sheriff's full designation is required on every official document. A sheriff assigned to court duty is referred to as Deputy Sheriff for Courtroom Protocol. The court recorders' official documentation includes everything done or said in court proceedings. *Um*s and *ah*s are also recorded in the documents. I didn't realize how many *um*s and *ah*s had come out of me until I read one of my testimonies. Frankly, even I had a problem believing anything I said, there were so many of them! Thank goodness I didn't fart—I'd hate to think how they would have recorded that.

The memories involving the sheriffs over the years are many. Now and then I was razzed or tricked to see my reaction or just to liven up a depressing day with a laugh. I do not blush easily—never have—but I think it may have been a goal that a few of the "little dickens" tried to make happen by comical incidents.

At one point a sheriff hobbled into my office after lunch complaining of a sore leg. He said he must have twisted it on the stairs or something but he really needed it examined. I had him sit down and, without having him strip down to his skivvies, began to check his lower leg for swelling and inflammation through his uniform. Unbeknownst to me, an interested audience was gathering outside the half-open door to be in on the fun.

"Oh, no, that's not where it hurts. It's higher up," he said. Obediently I moved my hands to his knee, and then a bit higher, only to encounter a stiff sausage-shaped mass running down along the inside of his leg. "Ahhhh, that's it!" he exclaimed with a groan of relief.

At my shocked expression he roared with laughter and pulled out a sock he'd stuffed with toilet paper and suspended from the waistband of his slacks. What can you do but laugh at yourself in a situation like that?

A couple of initiations were laid on new full-time sheriffs and on auxiliary sheriffs as well. Nothing dangerous like hanging them from the Lions Gate Bridge in a Volkswagen—that was the U.B.C. engineers.

On one memorable occasion in 1980 a new auxiliary escort sheriff (I'll call him Randall because I like the name), who was partnered with an experienced sheriff driver, asked Control to open the secure court bay door so the van could enter. What he didn't know was that there were about eight sheriffs and myself crammed around the escort monitor to watch the drama unfold.

The dispatcher informed Randall that the bay door required a particular security protocol to open. Now, this lad was young and eager to follow instructions during his orientation. Randall was instructed by the dispatcher to exit the escort vehicle and commence rubbing a three-foot steel marker post located by the van door. The instructions were explicit. He was to rub the pole with a vigorous movement of both hands from top to bottom and the door would open.

The fellow proceeded to apply the requested action to the pole "genie" but radioed Control that the door was not opening. Control then instructed the poor guy to rub briskly with one hand and pat the top of the post with the other.

When the instructions had been carried out, the door rolled up. Randall arrived in the escort control office to applause, pats on the back and an awful lot of "gotcha" laughter. He is still living it down after many years of service!

Another favourite initiation involved an R.C.M.P. supervisor requesting certified copies of new sheriffs' bare footprints for their identity files. The compliant sheriffs removed boots and socks and rolled up their uniform pant legs, sitting on a chair with their feet resting on their heels while the fingerprint officer rolled ink over the soles and toes of both feet. Photos were taken at various stages of the process to accompany the actual prints obtained when the sheriffs stood on white copy paper.

The police supervisor, the new sheriff and a witness then signed the "document" and it was officially stamped.

I know of one sheriff in another jurisdiction who asked why this was required since his fingerprints were on file. He accepted the explanation that if his hands were traumatized so his fingerprints were not accessible, the footprints would serve as back-up identification, just like the footprints taken from newborn infants.

This particular sheriff returned from his lunch break and saw the control office window decorated with Polaroid pictures and fax copies of the officially signed footprints. The headline above said, "P—, you have just been had by your fellow sheriffs and police officers!"

I knew the fax had been sent to all sheriff depots in the province of British Columbia. I received a copy in Vancouver. This sheriff is still very dear to me!

Only one time in all those many years did I play Cupid and helped to arrange a tea break because I felt that it was a meeting meant to happen. The deputy was a young, sweet and respectful gentleman. The young lady was also sweet and a very nice girl. She was a Mental Patients' Association (M.P.A.) worker in the courthouse.

The deputy certainly noticed her and wanted to know her name. He wondered whether I would help with an introduction. Normally I would not be a party to the dating game—I knew that "boys will be boys." This introduction was unique: a wonderful guy and a wonderful girl. I was happy to see what I could do.

The M.P.A. worker had no idea who the deputy was, even though I described him pretty well, and she didn't recognize his name. Still, they met for a coffee break and about three days later, he left a Valentine's Day rose on her desk. They started dating and became engaged two years later.

I was so happy to be a featured guest on their wedding day. They are now the wonderful parents of two beautiful teenage daughters.

Many sheriffs grew up with me and I saw them marry, become parents and watched their children grow up through pictures. I felt like a surrogate Grandma to many of their kids.

Five:
Who, What, Where

I will try to explain who we housed in cells #1 to #10 in the basement, to help you understand the wide variety of people we dealt with on a daily basis. The system probably still works this way.

Control was a desk surrounded by tempered glass. Only when there were no prisoner movements in progress would Control give clearance so the nurse and other sheriffs could make safe use of the stairs, elevator or main entry to accommodate cell or lawyer interviews. The Court Sheriff alerted the Control Sheriff by radio when prisoners were being moved from the courthouse to the holding cells and vice versa. The Control Sheriff constantly monitored prisoner movement using cameras.

Cell #1 was the first stop for all male prisoners arriving from the V.P.D. in the "city bucket." It was a temporary holding cell only. Prisoners were taken out to be searched by cell sheriffs (often assisted by court sheriffs if the numbers were large... thirty or more some days) and moved into Cell #5. Cell #1 also acted as a secure holding location for escort sheriff loads for court and returns to institutions, or for federal immigration officer pick ups for immigration court hearings.

Cells #2 and #6 were what we called piggyback cells. Cell #2 was a small secure holding area gated for entry and exit to Cell #6, a crowded temporary cell. Cell #2 allowed us to call out provincial prisoners individually (like an airlock) for continuation of their court appearances. We didn't want to have forty or so prisoners decide to exit Cell #6 *en masse* for control reasons—we'd have had to change our underwear if that happened! Cell #6 held provincial prisoners serving two years less a day who were appearing on another charge, and remanded prisoners who were continuing their court appearances during trial.

Cell #3 was a time-out "telephone booth" cell for an aggressive prisoner. There was no toilet or bench, but a very authentic looking pay phone and candy bar machine were painted on the wall when I first started at the courthouse. The cell was generally short-stay to manage a prisoner with a short fuse. As a side note, these paintings were removed from the walls around the same time as the Human Rights Act purged all sexually explicit reading materials and calendars from the holding cells. I'm not quite sure why.

Cell #4 was for federal prisoners (sentenced to more than two years) who were appearing on other court charges. Interestingly, many sentenced under provincial statutes requested the extra day so they could be held in a federal institution—repeat offenders mostly. This got them better food with less whining. Peace, bro!

Cell #5 housed people arrested by the V.P.D. on new charges. Their names were listed on the docket slate for first appearances on their charges. The accused must appear before a justice of the peace or a judge "in due course" (usually within forty-eight hours) under the Human Rights Act. People arrested by the city police or R.C.M.P. on an outstanding warrant or a new charge under provincial or federal statutes were also held in Cell #5 as newly arrested.

People arrested under federal warrants are classified as "in custody" under a federal warrant of apprehension. British Columbia deputy sheriffs must escort them to appear on charges originating in our province, including transporting people arrested in another area of Canada to B.C. Often we saw a domino effect involving several charges in other jurisdictions. The court in the area where the arrest was made dealt with the most recent charge. In some cases, the accused could transfer other charges to the same jurisdiction. The courts approved this procedure when the accused chose to plead guilty on charges from the other jurisdiction.

Otherwise sheriffs transported those charged to the court responsible for their outstanding warrants, if feasible. In general, the accused appeared in every area where he was charged, because he would require clearance from each of them prior to release on any outstanding charge. Even when the accused was given a release on another charge, he usually received a remand in custody order for charges in other jurisdictions.

Any outstanding charges or warrants for arrest in another province, as well as Canada-wide warrants, are always entered on the national police computer information system called C-PIC, pronounced "See-Pick." In my experience, the odd prisoner was released in error but the information was relayed quickly to the police so the person was often back in custody in a relatively short period of time. Sometimes the prisoner even turned himself in! The present computer system has streamlined accessibility to all information on all wanted people, provincial or federal. An error of release is highly unlikely due to this advanced technology.

Canada-wide warrants are generally for charges of a serious nature, such as murder, escape from custody on a federal charge, kidnapping, or a major drug-related charge. Immigration investigations also fall under this category.

Immigration officers execute immigration warrants at holding facilities and escort individuals to immigration hearings. If the immigration warrant stands, the immigration offender is held in one of the existing remand facilities as an immigration detainee until their status is clear. Some are detained for many years in Canada if the state or country where the offence occurred has the option to sentence the person to execution. Canada has no death penalty so our federal government is resistant to deporting someone to a location where the death sentence is a possibility.

A little digression here—my opinion is, who are we to interfere in another country's legal sentencing? The charge originated in another nation under their laws and statutes. Sentences in those countries are none of our business—ship them home!

We citizens shoulder a horrendous tax burden by housing offenders and interfering in the deportation process. For example, a man charged in Washington State for the execution-style murder of nine people in a gambling house was held in Calgary, Alberta for four to five years before he was deported. Washington State still has the death penalty.

In my opinion, if a Canadian offence on the books, deal with it and send the sucker back to where he came from. If the sentence of death is a possibility for the offence in that country, so be it.

It is interesting to note that the immigration warrant is one of the strongest documents in Canadian law. A person can be held in custody for an unspecified length of time. Immigration officers later transport them to a federal immigration hearing to discuss their status in Canada. In an immigration hearing the federal authorities thoroughly investigate the person's visa or other documents, the purpose of his stay and the nature of any questionable activities in Canada before granting either a release or an order of deportation. If evidence of other charges under provincial or federal statutes exists, the person must also appear in criminal court on those charges. Even if he obtains a release on the criminal charges he will not be released until cleared by immigration authorities.

Cell #6 held prisoners already in custody from Oakalla Institution in Burnaby or from institutions elsewhere in the province. These men were due in court for a variety of reasons and were housed separately from the V.P.D. load (yet another term I learned over the years—it means all those arrested since the last transfer the previous day from the police holding cells) because they had already been sentenced or had previously been ordered remanded in custody. Inmates housed in Cell #6 had been sentenced to incarceration anywhere from two or three days to two years less a day in a provincial correctional facility.

A few were housed alone in protective custody. The sheriffs, nurse or police could advise protective custody based on the nature of the offence, the inmate's status in custody or acute psychological problems that might compromise his safety while in court cells.

Prisoners who are given sentences of two years or more are held in federal institutions. There is a thirty-day appeal period during which time the sentenced person could remain in a remand facility, but the prisoner may opt out of the appeal and go directly to the institution. This is often the case when the court evidence is strong and an appeal is unlikely to alter the verdict.

Prisoners who may be facing charges under a provincial statute are also held as federal inmates if they have already been federally sentenced on another charge. Also, a surprising number of people sentenced to two years less a day will request additional time because they would rather be housed in a federal facility than a provincial one. It reminds me of the old song, "What a Difference a Day Makes!"

Cells #7 and #8 were protective custody cells. They were not monitored constantly but designated sheriffs made scheduled checks as posted.

Cell #9 was a long slanted hallway to house mentally ill or feisty prisoners. It featured easy access to Court 101. Little did the prisoners know that from there they could have punched a hole through the wall to an unused tunnel that passed under Cordova Street to the V.P.D. at 312 Main!

Cell #10 was off the hallway behind Court 101. It was used to house female prisoners designated for appearance in Court 101. The cell was not visible to male prisoners and had a toilet walled off for privacy. When a female finished her court appearance, she was moved up to the second-floor women's holding cell area (duty posted by two sheriffs, female or co-ed) if an extra cell was required for a male prisoner designated for Court 102, for transgender or transvestite prisoners, or for juvenile prisoners awaiting transfer to family court or juvenile detention centre.

Most prisoners remained in the court cells for upward of four hours before their court appearances. The judge then determined whether the prisoners would be released, remanded in custody or sentenced. It took a further several hours to process the paperwork from the courts and provide the documents to the #1 Sheriff Records Officer in the holding area. It was not uncommon for prisoners to wait up to eight hours at this stage.

The records officer is an extremely important person. All court documents pass through Records to determine and process the final papers required for release or detainment. For instance, if any other outstanding warrants from other jurisdictions existed or there was an immigration detainment order, the records officer contacted the relevant facility to clarify the holding documents.

No prisoners stayed overnight in the courthouse holding cells. If a question arose regarding a prisoner's paperwork, the prisoner was moved back to the Vancouver police holding cells until the papers were clarified or a justice of the peace saw the prisoner. (The justice of the peace determines whether the prisoner receives a Remand or Own Recognizance Release order in the absence of a judge. Their decisions are generally based on consultation with the Crown prosecutor and the defence attorney.)

The senior Vancouver police officer in charge of the V.P.D. holding cells also has a power of decision called a Promise to Appear (P.T.A.). The decision is based on the circumstances of the arrest and the prisoner's prior history of past offences. It requires plausible assurance that the accused will cooperate and appear in court to respond to the charge.

It was a new day every day: different faces, familiar faces, nice people and very naughty people. The total number of prisoners from everywhere averaged 150 a day. This number of prisoners did not include the court arrests—people arrested on outstanding warrants after they appeared in court on another charge. Some days we were up in the 200 range for total numbers in custody. Days like those were a gong show for everyone.

I recall the memorable arrest of a man who entered a bank and brandished a gun. His obvious intent was robbery. There were long line-ups in the bank on this particular day. Perhaps it was a payday.

The perpetrator pulled his weapon and approached the teller, demanding money. He was waiting for his demand to be met when he noticed that the customer at the wicket next to him, a man with a logger's build, had a large sum of paper currency in his hand.

The perpetrator made a grab for the money. The big guy made a motion to hand it over, and while the robber's eyes were on the cash he grabbed the gun and hit the robber over the head with it, then calmly made his deposit. The accused, with eight sutures in his head, arrived in our holding cells to a standing ovation (impartial, of course), just as a crowd applauds an injured player being taken off the field.

It was not uncommon for me to be dealing with a withdrawal seizure in the basement holding cells while being summoned to the fourth-floor court holding tier for another medical emergency. If the V.P.D. had carried out a drug bust or sting operation the previous day, it pretty well guaranteed a long, challenging day.

Physical combat between prisoners required duty sheriffs to undertake "cell extractions"—just like a tooth extraction, the rotten one had to come out. In this case the rotten one ended up in segregation in Cell #2 or #3. Often, the better part of a busy day's shift was spent squelching angry outbursts or managing prisoner behaviour, usually relating to drug deals.

All sheriffs could be called from any posting by radio code to go anywhere in the five-story building to intervene in incidents of various kinds, medical and physical. Control locked down all the holding areas, allowing no prisoner movement, until the problems were resolved. During lockdowns I was on stand-by, ready to be escorted to areas where people had sustained injuries. On one occasion a prisoner vanished from the windowless holding cell for the fifth floor courtroom. It was a classic mystery scenario, until the sheriffs figured out he had escaped into the ceiling vent ducting and was touring the fifth floor vent system. He took awhile to find!

Disruptive or combative individuals were often people appearing in court out of custody, fresh off the street. They might have been released on their charges out-of-custody but had been re-arrested outside the courtroom on an outstanding warrant of arrest for other charges. It sure pissed them off to be remanded in custody without their toothbrushes! I often administered a Jolly Rancher from my stock medication cupboard to calm them down.

Marginalized people were a very real problem in the public areas of the courthouse. These were people who fell through the cracks of Mental Health Services into the court justice system. Very often these unfortunate people had stopped taking their psychotropic medication. Their charges and arrests usually involved mischief or causing a disturbance. There is definitely some truth to the old wives' tales of the influence of a full moon. I am a lunar person and usually notice a change in myself. I just had to look at the sky or a celestial calendar to confirm it, which gave credibility to my howls for the day.

I must add at this point that we also received into custody some very polite, frightened, educated people who had gotten themselves into a jam of some kind. Their freedom was in jeopardy. Many were there for driving while impaired (D.W.I.) or had domestic problems; others had been arrested on federal charges such as expropriation of large sums of money or other white-collar crimes. Or they were arrested as johns of a working girl.

Once a year, we received a cell-load of turkeys. Literally! We looked forward to a quiet day with a different kind of turkey—one we could take home for Christmas dinner.

Corrections was often crowded at Christmas. The season was still special, and we were "family" to our regulars. We were what they needed at Christmas, a special time usually filled with loneliness and depression. Any place was better than the street during that season. Memories good and bad seemed to bombard the disadvantaged. Pain—emotional and physical—intensified at Christmas and being with others was so important. What better way for them to spend the festive season than to be with people who had known them for many years? The familiarity of our holding cells and a few days in a correctional facility helped them cope.

Many agencies provide consistent, dedicated services at Christmas for people like those, and their families. The volunteers give their time and toys from "Santa", and receive the gift of appreciation in return. It shows in the smiles at a wonderful Christmas dinner and hugs from people they know and trust.

Six:
Lookies, Listening and Chats

The V.P.D. nurses and I made daily phone calls to each other about medical issues or potential problems. Because of the sheer numbers of prisoners we dealt with, excellent communication both ways ensured problematic or complex health issues were out in the open so we were all aware of possible intervention or observation requirements.

We became good friends over the phone. It was neat to meet them when I was included in their Christmas parties, after many years of "good phone." We were all good nurses working in the anti-social side of nursing, united in respect for each other's expertise.

A few expressed surprise at my appearance. I had a laugh with one who said, "I only realized at the party who you were when I heard you say something. You looked too sweet and gentle with your white hair, to be Bonnie, the court cells' nurse."

I responded, "I am sweet and gentle. Now please pass the fucking salt."

Some of the V.P.D. nurses were Vancouver police officers, but all were designated as officers during their working hours.

The designation allowed them to conduct hands-on searches of female prisoners and manage rowdy prisoners of any gender more effectively.

The V.P.D. nurses were responsible for assessing all arrested and detained males and females. Their duties stretched them to the limit, as mine often did. We suffered overloaded days fraught with health issues, emergency interventions and management of noncompliant prisoners.

Every day was an adventure into the unknown. Some health issues slipped past without being detected by either V.P.D. officers or nurses. The numbers were just too large to keep track of and sometimes symptoms did not appear until several hours after arrest, depending on when they last used.

My responsibility as Sheriff's Nurse was to do a monitoring assessment upon each prisoner's arrival. Medication needed was determined at that time.

I learned very quickly that certain terms used by psychiatric professionals could be misconstrued. During a one-on-one assessment of a prisoner, I questioned a response by the inmate with the textbook statement, "You are trying to manipulate me." The prisoner's reply was, "I'm not even fucking touching you!" After that, phrases like "Don't play games," "Get serious," and "Not likely," became my usual verbal responses during medical history assessment. They were honest, comprehensible and made my expectations understood straight off the bat.

A common practice of prisoners, whether remanded or sentenced, was to exaggerate their drug abuse level. It was not uncommon for those charged to claim a heavy four-cap-a-day heroin habit so they could receive withdrawal medication while incarcerated. Still, if their physical symptoms did not jive with a heavy habit then the inmate got the "get serious" response.

Not only that, but if remand was to Vancouver Pre-trial on a busy day I went over to assist with intake there when my own work was done at 222. The look on a prisoner's face could be a Kodak moment. I think they thought I was stalking them from the court cells to detention. It might have been their worst nightmare, but it was straight up front and honest.

Prisoner: "I just saw you in the Court cells."

Me: "Oh, that was the other Bonnie." (Of course, the other Bonnie was either a sheriff or a payroll clerk!)

It was common practice for a prisoner to make requests for medication on arrival in our holding area. When this happened I made it very clear that they were in our facility to appear on their charges and not for their medical complaints. Still, I always assessed a complaint prior to their court appearances. I listened, observed and clarified priorities for the individual. It might be hospital or court, or even a return to V.P.D. at 312. Maybe they would get medication and maybe not—they would also be seen by a psychiatrist at Pre-trial.

It was very hard to remain neutral and non-judgmental if I was aware of the nature of the charges against prisoners in the cells. I preferred not to know. I just did my thirty or more head-to-toe assessments per day along with the verbal medical histories required for new intake prisoners fresh off the street, or following a remand or sentencing by the courts.

In most cases, it was better for me not to know the charges. I really did not want to hear that this person hated all women, particularly nurses, and was charged with thumping the hell out of one in a hospital parking lot. I guess he thought women had peed on his toothbrush at some time in his life. (This is an analogy, but maybe the physical act might have been an effective deterrent at a time when his attitude required adjustment.)

There I go again, back to bodily functions! All nurses seem to feel that elimination is a primary (but resolvable) problem. It seems uppermost in a nurse's mind that if the bowels are functioning, all other physical ills are cared for effectively. My mother was a registered nurse. If my brother or I had even a zit, she would suggest we park on the porcelain throne for a while. It's strange, but after we followed her medical advice, the zit dried up quite quickly. But I digress.

Yours truly often included the "F.O.S." classification on assessment transfer documents. Assessments served as an important part of admission to remand or sentencing to institution. It gave a heads-up to all those at the institution who were having to deal with the new inmate. For Joe and Jane Citizen, the acronym stands for "Full of Shit." The space on the document was insufficient for a comprehensive description of what the "problem" might be for the prisoner.

It was near kin to another entry coined by yours truly, "I.L.S." I.L.S. was a term I used to describe a skinny, swaggering "new fish." It was a shortened version of my visual assessment—Imaginary Lat Syndrome. In layman's terms it was the big-man-on-campus attitude. The syndrome was usually resolved, in some fashion, at the correctional facility. I.L.S. did not usually manifest its splendour on any future visits to our holding cells.

Don't feel ignorant for not understanding the short forms. Almost every nurse or other professional who saw one of my entries for the first time phoned me for clarification of the acronyms. The spaces on the document were very small. I had to be creative to fit the important information into it.

I, at least, knew that my assessments were read before filing, if only for a laugh. Personally I think my acronyms should be approved for forensic assessments, or the spaces made larger.

Shortened terminology such as *bid* (twice a day) and *tid* (three times a day) are standard terms used *prn*—that is, as needed—by all professionals in any area of health care. Why not these?

Time management is very important when you're facing twenty-five or more assessments a day. The receiving facility's staff could be properly prepared for the arrival of an a-hole remand in a very short time using the descriptive information in an assessment.

Because I served in the Crowbar Hotel longer than most lifers, my assessments were as close to word pictures as I could get. Nurses elsewhere always read my assessments. I was told they were like a picture book description: nothing derogatory or false, just factual observations at the time of my interview. Still, if the assessments were too clinical and lacked amusing or colourful content, they were less likely to be read thoroughly. The staff could miss important health alerts. But they read mine!

My purpose was not to deride the prisoner. It was my duty to inform the receiving facility of my assessment gained through questioning and observation. The approach proved to be a very effective communication tool.

My prime duty was to observe and report on the status of the prisoners' health. Duty nurses at the V.P.D. jail and the court nurse communicated daily. It was extremely important to have open communication regarding medical issues.

I wanted to be notified of potential health issues that could interfere with a charged person's court appearance. Health complications can be an unknown factor due to the volume of arrests on a long weekend's stay in the V.P.D. cells, when the police nurses might not have had time to assess every prisoner, or had not been informed about a problem.

The accused was in custody to have the charge heard in court or in the presence of a Justice of the Peace "in due course." Anything interfering with this process could be considered a violation of rights under the Criminal Code and could result in the judge dismissing the charges due to "unnecessary delay."

The J.P. would make personal visits to hospital when a prisoner's serious health problem prevented him from attending court. The J.P. had to determine whether the accused would be remanded in the hospital under correctional guard or would be released on his own recognizance to appear in court on a specified date. The accused are not in our holding cells for medical treatment; they are there to appear on a criminal charge. There have to be concrete and serious medical or psychological reasons to permit any diversion from appearing at court. Occasionally the prisoner's lawyer and sometimes I had to appear to clarify why the accused could not attend.

Sometimes detainees came in with injuries sustained during arrest. The K-9 service has a particular fancy for crotches and butts; basically, they are ordered into action and take perps down by their "members." Are you wincing yet? Those doggies sure fetched a lot of bones over the years! I dressed some very nasty injuries sustained by K-9 intervention and supplied the odd doughnut ring to sit on. Still, it is interesting to note that human bites have far more potential for infection than the ones supplied by the kibbles and bits squad.

The sheriffs were generally prompt to inform me if there were health issues noticed during transfers or prisoner pat-downs. A request for assessment could also come from the judge hearing the case, the lawyer for the accused or the court mental health worker. If we missed important information, it could compromise an individual's court appearance or affect staff or other prisoners' safety in our cells. I had to assess all information passed on.

I did not do feet or hangnails, but life-threatening situations required my attention. Very often these consisted of severe drug or alcohol withdrawal, Grand Mal epileptic seizures, physical trauma injuries or a medical history of heart trouble or diabetes.

Because prisoners did not remain with us after court hours were finished, and the transfers for court appointments did not occur until after breakfast, the only meal we had to deal with was lunch. Lunch in the holding cells consisted of a triple-decker sandwich of mystery meat and cheese, a cup of soup and coffee. We were often asked to provide special diets for diabetes or other conditions, which we always adhered to. But if the diet requested was vegetarian, my instruction to the prisoner was usually, "Take out the meat!"

We often "enjoyed" the company of high-profile prisoners, some of whom were extremely demanding. One in particular stands out. This murderer was the King Asshole while he was in our court cells. He thrived on notoriety and on manipulating our judicial system. A high profile childkiller who made many demands for preferential treatment during his trial, he used his notoriety to receive special treatment while in custody.

I recall him demanding a special meal due to a claimed medical condition. I did not find any such problem during my clinical assessment, so I contacted Oakalla, where he was being held until his trial was finished, and was informed by the nurse that special dietary issues were not indicated at the institution's hospital unit. While he was in the court cells he received the same food as the other prisoners. He did, however, dine alone. Many prisoners expressed a desire to have him lodged with them in their holding cells. I wonder why?

Sheriff Court Services is an impartial entity of the justice system. Still, when his verdict was given and his thirty-day appeal period ended, he was relocated to a federal institution, where he remains to this day—over thirty-five years later. He certainly loved seeing his name in ink then, and he still does. It seems that every time he did so much as pick his nose it was in the newspapers. I believe he has earned a few advanced education diplomas at taxpayers' expense, but I don't wish him to see his name in my book.

Institutions sent prisoners' medication with the escorting sheriffs for continuity while in our cells. It generally consisted of physician-ordered antibiotics or seizure management preparations, which I administered as prescribed. The street nurse for sexually-transmitted disease (S.T.D.) control also visited the city holding cells every weekday to maintain disease tracking continuity in the community. I worked in friendship with the same nurse, Liz James, for over twenty years. Everyone respected her dedication—prisoners, nurses and the community at large—and I appreciated not being the only golden oldie around.

My duty was to determine that the person was "fit for court." Fitness was based on physical health and mental capability to understand the charge and to instruct a defence lawyer. If the prisoner's health required immediate intervention I often had to appear in front of a judge to clarify why the prisoner could not appear. Medical diversion from court had to be supported by strong need: life or death. The health issue took precedence over appearance.

I had to do a particularly thorough assessment now and then to eliminate Academy Award performances by inmates. I would be dishonest if I said I was never fooled. I was at times. However, I did develop certain assessment techniques that gave credible results along with a few laughs.

If I determined that a male prisoner was faking a seizure, I used to announce that I needed a pain response from the inmate to assess his L.O.C. (level of consciousness). I then instructed the sheriff accompanying me to open the man's zipper so I could pull his pubic hair.

The first few times I said that the sheriff looked at me with a shocked expression. But the request worked every time, resulting in a fast recovery well-oriented as to person, place and time. I never had to tug on the curlies.

B.T.B. (back to bowels) yet again. Occasionally I determined that an old-school nurse's solution would allow the inmate to "strive toward a compliant attitude" while in our custody. Being a forensic nurse, I was fond of recommending enema procedures as a placebo treatment for negative attitudes. In some cases just the mere description of the "Three-H" proved to be markedly effective to attain compliance. The definition of this particular medical intervention is "high, hot, and a helluva lot." It is amazing how effective it is for making brown eyes blue! It's a bit of a far out analogy but I'm sure it gives you a word picture of the effectiveness of the described procedure in focusing the possible recipient. In severe cases, perhaps an equipment alteration (of the garden hose variety in the appropriate orifice and the hot tap full on and bubbling) would have resulted in a stalwart, law-abiding citizen if it had been administered in the "nuclear meltdown" teenage years.

I never followed through with the treatment in jail but I spoke street language fluently enough that the inmate understood my interpretation of his response or his request. On the other side of the coin, Jolly Rancher candies or red licorice twists were administered frequently to acknowledge prisoner compliance.

I was straight up with the prisoners and I expected the same in return. "Never shy away or placate" was a motto I lived by and practised every day. It was important to develop honesty and trust with the people I cared for, and I truly cared about them. A laugh, a shoulder to cry on or a hug for encouragement were always available as indicated.

Chats took place in my small office with a sheriff at the door. These confidential meetings had the purpose of providing empathy, reassurance and a reminder to Phone Your Mom. One particular young man was reminded each time he "joined us for lunch" and would report back to me on his return, "Bonnie, I phoned Mom and she said Hi to you." Sadly, this sweet lad passed away suddenly. I attended his memorial service and was re-united, tearfully, with his mom and dad. It turned out that some forty-five years earlier we had been high school friends.

I never said anything demeaning to inmates who needed to talk about their fears and regrets. I provided company, an ear and a safe place to cry for some of the toughest inmates we handled over the years. Giving them the freedom to lower the façade and talk about feelings, regrets and hope often inspired me to go to work each day.

There's not much peer acceptance for tears and fear in a jail. It was not a place for girly-man emotions, but tears were allowed during my assessments, or in private chats. They are emotional expressions of loss and regret. Caring, encouragement and trust from somebody just might open the door a crack to effecting changes in lifestyle and attitude. I made time to listen for those precious minutes. I never ignored an opportunity for a possible change of heart or direction.

I have known many of the incarcerated for many years—in the holding cells, in the corrections environment and on the streets where they lived and died. Up to three generations in turn would invite me to enter their space to listen without judgement.

There were very few who did not thank me or hug me on the street. Hugs were free and so was my encouragement, stressing a glass-half-full approach. I recall a guy crying because he'd slipped in his recovery. I then said, "Yes, but how long were you clean?" It turned out he'd been clean three months. I focused on the positive and said, "Okay, clean three months and you slipped once. That means you can do at least another three months!"

Still, in every occupation there are bad hair days, and mine was no exception. One extremely busy and stressful day I was bothered by one regular prisoner's requests for Tylenol and Gravol. Every time I walked past the cell he asked for medication: "Nurse, I need Tylenol and Gravol." I reminded him, politely, of the six-hour rule for medication. The city police nurses had no information about when and what he had used prior to his arrest, so we gave no medication at all for the first six hours in custody, after which the prisoner was reassessed. It was a strict protocol we followed with our daily transfer information.

He ate a good lunch and I noted no withdrawal symptoms. Finally, after hearing his demands hour after hour, I stopped at the cell and made it perfectly clear in a strong, loud voice, "Listen, normally I carry Tylenol, Gravol and fuck all. I am out of Tylenol and I am out of Gravol, so what does that leave you?" A loud chorus of prisoners replied in unison, "Fuck all!" The ensuing uproarious laughter (including the inmate's) was the best medicine for everyone on that particular day.

My explanation became renowned, although I only used it the one time in frustration. It caused much laughter from the many professionals who got wind of it. It certainly was deemed to be an effective communication tool and even appeared on my retirement wishes card about ten years later. Some physicians in Corrections have told me that they still make use of the explanation, *prn*, to this very day. Knowing the people I worked alongside, and other contacts in my career, the phrase might very well be etched on my tombstone. God forgive me!

I must assure you that I carefully assessed any physical complaints and noted the results. Some street drugs have a delayed effect. More often than not street drugs are contaminated, cut with toxic substances. Rat poison was a common ingredient. The user was often aware of the cut but used it anyway because it enhanced the high.

Seven:
Rollin', Rollin', Keep Those Wagons Rollin'

In the B.C. Penitentiary days, a sheriff transport bus carried a large number of federal inmates to and from federal facilities and our holding cells. The bus's capacity was fifty-two inmates, and the daily norm was to make two trips at capacity to and from the courts, one morning and one afternoon. It often took three trips because of protective custody and gender situations. These numbers did not include arrested people from the city cells at 312 Main Street, people who were arrested in court on a P.T.A. or female inmates from Lakeside Correctional Centre or the Twin Maples provincial facility (jokingly referred to as "Twin Nipples" by sheriff escorts) in Maple Ridge. Three sheriffs were required on the bus: two in front and one riding shotgun in the back.

Male federal prisoners waiting out their thirty-day appeal period, and all provincial prisoners, were housed in Oakalla. The bus had several separate compartments but that didn't help with the noisy comments and threats of violence. Some of the trips were the "get out of Dodge" type, featuring a hurried radio call for correctional back-up upon arrival at the facility if a fight broke out among prisoners. In all cases escorts reported in-transit prisoner altercations to the court cells, escort dispatch and the institutions.

The sheriff warned the prisoners verbally about any unacceptable behaviour or scuffles, and non-compliant inmates were brought under control by subtle forms of aversion therapy. Now and then the driver had to avoid the odd dog or cat en route. Such quick movements saved the animal, with a bonus—it made a great deterrent and prisoner attitude adjustment tactic.

In some cases, animal avoidance on the road was the only option deputies had available to manage prisoners' actions on a particular day. Diversions were never taken to the extent of causing personal injury. It was a "shuffling the deck" tactic only.

The escort vehicle never stopped in transit without R.C.M.P. backup and escort clearance. Hey, we are talking about high profile prisoners: murderers and perpetrators of intolerable crimes against society with nothing to lose—no way do two escort sheriffs open the van door just to break up a scuffle.

In some situations I applied a few band-aids and dispensed Jolly Ranchers to cranky inmates in the wagon bay when the bus arrived. I also wrote a few incident reports citing "no evidence of physical injuries noted on assessment of all prisoners." Some prisoners see dollar signs and may sue for injuries sustained while being transported, so documentation was a C.Y.A. for both the escorts and me.

Most prisoners adhered to the code of silence among inmates— "I know nothing about who, what or where." An eyeball could be hanging out of his head and a prisoner's response would be, "It just fell out..." That is the power of the code among prisoners. Besides, those damn dogs the van had to avoid should have been on a leash under owners' control in the first place!

The sheriffs kept radio contact with Escort Control to consult with management and identify resolution strategies should violence or medical issues threaten during a trip. Back-up included other law enforcement agencies in the geographic area involved. Safety for all was paramount in the decision process.

We sometimes got a hint from newspapers or radio news regarding an arrest by the police. Police officers or nurses prepared us for the arrival of individuals displaying unpredictable behaviour or medical concerns in advance, and we reciprocated. We were all wary of the unknown factor, which kept safety in the forefront of everyone's mind.

I would receive a packet listing people slated for court from the commissionaire when I picked up my keys every morning. A handwritten list of new male and female prisoners arrived every morning from 312. I also got a list from the sheriff escorts outlining who was expected to arrive from which institutions. These were lists of people in custody appearing on remand for an ongoing trial or *voir dire*, and noted each person who had a history of management precautions, medical or otherwise. These people might be appearing before a provincial court judge or would be transported by sheriffs from our cells to the Supreme Court holding cells at Howe and Smithe.

There is no jury in provincial court. The accused may elect for trial by jury at the Supreme Court only. I was consulted now and then regarding health problems in the Supreme Court cells. The escort sheriffs would take me to Supreme Court to assess, consult or treat and then they would return me to the bowels of "222 Maim Street."

The majority of prisoners in the cells were addicts experiencing withdrawal from narcotics, barbiturates, Talwin and Ritalin (known as T&R on the street) or, of course, alcohol. The T&R combination of drugs was very popular in the '60s and '70s, producing the ups

(Ritalin) and downs (Talwin) that users craved. Many of them abused multiple substances. Abusing inhalants such as glue, Varsol, Sterno, gasoline and nail polish remover was common in that particular era. Glue sniffing was just shy of endemic among youth from dysfunctional families of abusers or due to the ever-present peer pressure.

Inmates in institutions have access to a remarkable abundance of illicit drugs. Drugs arrived in the facility in ways that are difficult to believe possible, like in the core of a tennis ball thrown over the exercise yard wall, tucked away in a body cavity that cannot be searched by anyone except a physician, or even braided into a young child's hair on Open Family Visiting Day. The once-a-month open visit pretty well guaranteed that sixty percent of the females in the sentenced unit at Lakeside would be stoned that same evening on the drugs secreted on child visitors. Drugs were also stuck under tables with chewing gum and hidden by the inmate before the guards did their room sweep. The small children were not aware that drugs were hidden on them because many were under the age of six, and children of that age were not searched in those days.

The drugs arriving in institutions often have greater addictive properties than drugs on the street. They are more potent and people are in vulnerable circumstances. People may in fact become addicts while in prison.

A person, especially someone who is already marginalized, can enter a correctional facility straight and be released wired on heroin or amphetamines. Vulnerable people pay with cigarettes or sexual favours while in custody or cooperative obligations when released, and predatory criminals with access to drugs often take advantage of this.

Alcohol created a major management problem. It has always been the most abused and destructive legal drug available, destroying families at all levels of society and killing many innocent people on our roads. It causes havoc and heartache in our civilized society at large and presents a very difficult policing problem. There is no line between rich or poor. The Liquor Control Board (L.C.B.) is a cash cow so we are all the victims of the irresponsible logic of our government.

Alcohol abuse is Russian roulette for the innocent person caught in the middle. It is a no-win situation for families or victims. Too often, our courts accept the excuse of alcohol intoxication for road deaths or domestic violence. The "I was intoxicated and didn't have control" defence is true but where is the responsibility and where are the consequences?

Courts are too lenient in sentencing offenders. I have actually seen a person released on his own recognizance leave the court-house, get into a car with a passenger and drive it away himself, in blatant disregard of the judge's ruling. The police had seized this person's driver's license when he was charged for drunk driving and resisting arrest. The car he was driving when charged had been impounded.

An intoxicated person at the wheel of a vehicle is an armed and dangerous offender. The effect is no different than that of a "smoking gun"—dead is still dead. The victim and family are empty and grieving while the consequence for an offender is often a slap on the wrist and a "Naughty-naughty."

By the way, I have heard parents say how thankful they were that their youngster was charged under the influence of alcohol and not marijuana. I have yet to hear of a charge being laid for driving under the influence of marijuana. The charge today would likely be driving under the influence of an unknown substance unless drunk driving is confirmed through a breathalyser and subsequent blood tests.

Where is the justice? It is in the thin budget provided by government for mandatory bail supervision, driving suspensions and community service.

Monitoring by ankle bracelet, applied and monitored by a correctional facility, is a court decision based on the history of the accused and nature of the charge. They may be used when a sentence is pending so the person can continue to work.

The hours of detainment, when monitored prisoners must be at home under house arrest, and strict supervision requirements are part and parcel of the judge's decision. The judge also considers whether the convicted is a danger to himself or others. It is not a fail-safe deterrent, but it is effective for many offenders convicted of white-collar crimes or minor charges and eases the overcrowding situation in correctional facilities.

I should probably mention some of the institutions we worked with at the courthouse. I've already mentioned the local police departments, but prisoners from as far away as Agassiz might be sent to us as well. Agassiz Mountain Prison in the boonies housed men serving time for sex-related crimes and other heinous charges that may have affected their safety in the general population of other prisons. This facility bore the slang name of "Agony Mountain" in the olden days.

I want to go into a little history about the B.C. Penitentiary, or as it was known, the Pen. The B.C. Penitentiary in New Westminster was still open to federal prisoners in the late '70s, when I started at the courthouse. It was a heavily guarded facility that had never to my knowledge been updated to code, whatever that may be. It was home to the some of the most dangerous offenders in our society. I saw most of these dudes in our cells over the years. While it was not by any means state of the art in corrections by the time it was closed, the Pen did give us the opportunity to transfer federal prisoners to and from the courts more cost effectively and with less stress (for escort staff and prisoners).

This antiquated structure took up prime acreage in New Westminster overlooking the Fraser River. The only remaining structure today is the formidable main administration building. It has even been designated as historic, a commanding structure standing amid beautiful homes and townhouses. The lawns and garden are well maintained by the city. Unfortunately the warden's home on the property is gone. It was a wonderful example of its time, with gables, verandas and handcarved columns.

The federal government conducted public tours before a wrecking ball reduced the Pen to rubble in the early 1980s. It was an educational but frightening experience to be guided through the towers, cell tiers, guardhouses and walkways that made up its foreboding perimeter. The echo of voices and clatter of shoes on the cold concrete added a haunting reality check during the tours. The guide told visitors of many memorable happenings that were a part of the prison's story, significant events covering more than a hundred years.

The gallows were still standing, although I believe the last hanging was in the mid-1950s. Capital punishment was later abolished in Canada when the federal statutes pertaining to sentencing were revised.

A convicted murderer once told me that while he was on parole he visited his old cell on a public tour at the (closed) B.C. Pen. He said he wanted to see if his etchings were still on the cell walls. All I could think of at the time was that his actions remain etched in the memory of families left devastated by his murders—many of the victims were tortured prior to their deaths. One of his victims was an angelic, blond, blue-eyed nine-year-old boy. I saw my son's nine-year-old face in the picture of that little boy; it was difficult at times to set aside personal feelings from professional responsibility. Still, I imagine he has some new etchings on the walls of his present (and hopefully permanent) home.

During the tour the Pen still showed visible evidence of the destruction that followed a mass inmate riot in 1975. It was a sinister reminder of how latent violence can trigger a recessive gene in a human being who lacks the presence of a contrary gene in his genetic map.

A sociopath personality normally lacks or has not developed the required "contrary gene" of control. The genetic lack or defect can be triggered quite quickly. Circumstances of a relatively minor nature are often all it takes to initiate an explosive response. The result is a chain reaction that develops into a riot.

We have seen examples of this following sporting events, rock concerts and political demonstrations in our so-called civilized society. The infusion of irrational behaviour, combined with violent reprisal, is often triggered by a few and develops into a melee. The non-functional contrary gene shows up under peer influence and, in many cases, the added fuel of "L.K. Hall." Yes, home-brew was often available in the Pen, as it is in many institutions.

How volatile sentenced inmates can be was evident in the B.C. Pen riot of 1975. Many people do not even know what primary incident caused the riot. It possibly began with a complaint over the quality or quantity of food. It certainly gave credibility to the theory of latent gene dysfunction. Simmering anger among prisoners required only a minor irritation to evolve into a very dangerous domino effect between prisoners and staff. The eventual result of the 1975 fray was destruction of property and trauma injury.

A psychiatric nurse I knew was a prison counsellor at the B.C. Pen. She was a senior classmate of mine in the '60s and was respected by all. Her dedication and her ability to conduct communication sessions with inmates prior to pre-community release programs was beyond question. Corrections Canada supervised the assessments she completed and the behaviour of the inmates in these programs. The inmate participants had to adhere to specific guidelines to develop a positive attitude based on honesty and proven trustworthiness before community release.

We lost a beautiful, respected professional the day of the riot. She died of gunshot trauma. To me, she is a symbol of all innocent people caught in the middle of mayhem. There was never an intention on anyone's part that she fall victim to the violence that day. Inmates and staff shed tears together.

Eight:
You Need Only One
Muscle to Smile

It wasn't all doom and gloom. Sometimes humour happened.

I was driving to work one morning and was pulled over by a lurking R.C.M.P. officer for exceeding the speed limit on Barnet Highway. I knew I was busted. I lowered my window as the officer approached and smilingly asked, "I guess you're not stopping me to sell me tickets to the Policemen's Ball?" He immediately replied, "We don't have balls." As soon as the words left his lips he closed his ticket book, returned to his vehicle and left—without meeting my eyes once!

It took me some time afterward to compose myself and continue driving. Once I got to work I told the story to the sheriffs, who passed it on to the Burnaby sheriffs so they could get a laugh out of it too.

In the olden days of the '70s and '80s, we dealt with charges ranging from mischief to murder and just about every offence in between. We had many "regulars" in the cells. Some were in custody several times in a two-week period and gave us many opportunities for relief in laughter.

A man I will refer to as Harry was well-known to police, sheriffs, nurses, doctors and pretty much anyone working in mental health related fields (not to mention the businesses) between 4th Avenue on the west side of Vancouver and Gore Street on the east side. Harry was a flower child from the '60s. He loved West 4th Avenue: it was a colourful area of funky shops, natural and organic food stores and unique little stores that displayed an array of handicrafts, including lots of tie-dyed shirts and the linen homespun apparel that had been so popular among the hippies. Harry told me that he had "lived or crashed there for over twenty years." It was home to him. Harry even worked in a few restaurants on 4th when he was stable on his medication and his court-ordered geographic restrictions had been lifted.

Predictably unpredictable behaviour was the hallmark of our Harry. I met this memorable individual on my first day on the job—his antics varied depending on the length of time he had been off his medication.

It may seem strange, but we knew that if Harry was seen downtown, he would be in our cells within a day—often the same day! He was seldom in our geographic area when he was on his medication, but when he decided he did not need his pills he was a mere hoot and a holler away. Literally!

One day I was enjoying a coffee and my usual two doughnuts in the crowded court cafeteria. Harry, who was often banned from the cafeteria for his mischievous ways, appeared in the doorway. He summoned me loudly after spotting me sitting in a quiet corner.

The lobby commissionaire approached him and urged him away from the entrance. Good old unpredictable Harry responded in a very loud voice, "I have to see the nurse! She's carrying my child!"

A few days later he was being a general nuisance in the trendy 4th Avenue area. The merchants and residents needed a rest from

Harry—at least for a day or so. The V.P.D. laid a charge of mischief in a public place along with a "no-go" violation (Harry had been banned from West 4th after too many shenanigans). Empathy for the merchants on 4th prompted the arresting officer to lay a further charge under an unfamiliar felony Criminal Code number.

The records sheriff had held her position for a long time and could almost quote the Criminal Code from cover to cover, but this citation was not at all familiar to her. It required a detailed search in the statutes to identify it. It turned out to be the reference code for cattle rustling! Interesting, considering the area of arrest was West 4th and Yew Street, a Harry no-go area and generally a cow-pie-free zone.

As an aside, I wonder if that code is still on the books? Perhaps our government has established a committee for review, but I think a prompt swipe of Liquid Paper could remove the statute without spending tax dollars on a study committee.

Anyway, nobody was surprised when the judge released Harry after the prosecutor read the charges. He was given the usual no-go restriction and maybe instructed to leave the cows where they belonged. Thus residents and restaurants on 4th Avenue had a short break from Harry's nuisance behaviour. It also gave us all a bit of a laugh—even Harry, who stayed with us for soup and a sandwich, courtesy of the courthouse.

I always knew when Harry was on the load from the V.P.D. The loud greeting on his arrival was, "Nurse, I need my Lithium." He certainly did, but I didn't have any. Most of us might have benefited from a Valium by the end of a day with our Harry but I didn't have any of those either.

Harry also provided entertainment of sorts in the courtroom. It usually came unexpectedly and brought a smile or stifled laugh from the court. I even observed one of the judges lowering his face to the bench to smile.

On one particular day, the sheriff took Harry into the docket. The judge asked, "Do you have counsel, Mr. Jones?" Harry replied, "No, I just fired the S.O.B."

The judge said sternly, "These are rather serious charges, Mr. Jones."

Harry quickly replied, "I just hired the S.O.B. back." In the barely fifteen seconds this exchange took, the duty counsel lawyer returned to Harry's side in the prisoner's docket.

Sometimes Harry handled his own defence, doing his own cross-examination of the arresting police officer. On one occasion Harry chose to represent himself on a charge involving a breach of his no-go area on 4th Avenue. The Crown called the police officer to the stand, and the prosecutor proceeded to read the circumstances around the arrest.

I should note a point of courtroom protocol here: when someone is on the stand for questioning relating directly to a charge, responses are to be directed to the judge. The eye-to-eye contact assists the judge in assessing the credibility of the witness. The only exception is when the witness is asked to point to and verbally identify the accused.

Now back to Harry. The prosecutor finished his summary and Harry proceeded with his cross-examination.

Harry asked the officer, "In your report, you stated that I was on 4th Avenue. Is that a true statement?"

The officer replied to the judge, "Yes, that is a true statement, Your Honour."

Harry then asked the officer, "Is it not true that I was not on 4th Avenue, but that I was, in fact, on the roof overlooking 4th Avenue and you arrested me on 3rd Avenue?"

The officer kept a straight face and his eyes on the judge, and stated, "Yes, that is true, Your Honour."

Harry won a dismissal on that one but the officer didn't mind. Not only was he out-logicked fair and square, he was on overtime, making big bucks that day.

Harry was an erudite individual who spoke in an elegant, almost pompous manner. It seems that he'd fried his brain on L.S.D. and other psychedelics in the '60s. He was left in a chronically manic state following many years of drug abuse.

Harry spent one of his better days in custody scrubbing his cell with a toothbrush—a new one of course. The toothbrush was destroyed by his labours but it was a nice quiet day for us. I would recommend this approach to parents as a method to quiet noisy kids home from school on a rainy day. It just might work—for one day anyway. "Gather ye rosebuds while ye may... "

When Harry was in Oakalla and stable on his medication, he was obsessive compulsive for cleanliness and worked as a cleaner in the Oakalla hospital unit. He was a very soft and gentle man when his manic depressive psychosis was controlled by his prescribed Lithium.

He also enjoyed working in the Oakalla gardens. I imagine he had a bonding experience with weed in his past and kept the garden in a manicured state as a tribute to the "fatties" he remembered. He may even have tried to grow "bud" among the corn—good camouflage!

He was well monitored by the M.P.A. (Mental Patients Association) when out of custody and I'm almost positive that he was a charter member of I.M.P.S. (Inter-Ministerial Program Service). It was an elite program meant to help manage a particular group of clients who often posed a nuisance problem in the community and, at times, posed a threat to safety. Participants were seen on a regular basis (if they were complying) as ordered by the court, in the same way a person would be ordered to see a bail supervisor. The difference between the two was that I.M.P.S.

staff were experienced mental health counsellors associated with the justice system.

Harry also loved flowers, and on several occasions he would come by to bring me some—roots, dirt and all still clinging to the stalks. It confirmed to me that his heart was in the right place. It also gave me a heads up that his heart—and the rest of him—would be visiting us for lunch soon. I was usually right! Harry often decided to stop taking his medication. The result was usually an arrest for a misdemeanour of some kind.

On one particular occasion, Harry came into the building and asked if the sheriff escorts would give him a ride to Burnaby to appear on a charge. The escort sheriff made it clear that out-of-custody clients could not be transferred in a duty vehicle to another jurisdiction. Harry left the courthouse, crossed the street and threw a rock through the window of Human Resources Services. He was promptly arrested. When he arrived in our cells he said, "Now can I have a ride to Burnaby?"

I could write a whole book on Harry alone but I will close with an all-time favourite Harry story. I often sat in the courthouse gallery for Harry's appearances, to expedite the court decision documents. It was usually in everyone's best interest, Harry's included, to rush his paperwork so he could be released or transferred by escorts.

He was in custody again for his usual no-go on 4th. In his own cross-examination, Harry asked the officer, "Is it not true that you arrested me and put me in your police car and took me for a ride?" The officer replied, "Yes, that is true, Your Honour." Harry then asked the officer, "Is it not true that you took me for a ride in the *trunk* of your police car?" There was a marked pause and then the officer replied to the judge, "Yes, that is true, Your Honour."

The court stood down while the judge considered his decision. I think it required a break for all of us to regain our composure. I do not recall His Honour's decision on that day but I will always remember the details.

Another fellow I will call Billy was also on the Mental Patients Association's (M.P.A's) list when housed at the courthouse. One day Harry came in on the load from Oakalla wearing his prison greens. Billy had been arrested the night before and had come over from 312 Main.

On this particular day we had a shortage of single cells due to the sheer number of prisoners. Harry was usually held in protective custody in a single cell at court because he pissed off the other cons with his manic behaviour. Harry was appearing for setting fires in dumpsters and Billy was known for plugging cell toilets with rolls of toilet paper, thus causing flooding. I suggested the two be housed together. Problem solved! Harry could start a fire and Billy could put it out. The sheriffs put them in the same cell, and there were no fires or floods that day.

When it came time to do the paperwork the sheriff noted that Billy was wearing Harry's Oakalla greens and Harry had on Billy's suit. Harry proudly announced that he'd gotten the suit "with a song and a b.j."

Nine:
Girls and "Girls"

Give me ten male prisoners to care for over one female prisoner any day. Thank goodness the senior officer in charge of city cells released most of the females arrested by the police on a promise to appear (P.T.A.).

I'm sure you can guess the type of female that did arrive in our cells. Yeppers, la crème de la crème! The girls in our court cells were the worst of the worst in attitude and charges. Many were repeat offenders like their male counterparts and were often arrested with their johns or pimps. We usually received between eight and ten women daily from the city bucket and normally about the same number from Female Corrections.

The "cat house" was appropriately named for the screaming and fighting that went on in it. The potential for unpredictable violence often smouldered close to the surface, but firm female sheriffs along with yours truly, Nurse Ratched, were ready for the tough broads. The sheriffs had batons, handcuffs and pepper spray. I was fully armed with Jolly Ranchers. The sheriffs never used any of their accessories but I sure used a lot of Jolly Ranchers.

The "cat house cells" were located in the holding areas on the second floor of the courthouse. In-custody female prisoners from V.P.D. numbered up to twenty-five on a bad day, such as when the V.P.D. had done a round-up sting on the Stroll. The women were housed separately from the female prisoners from Lakeside Correctional Centre for Women.

We were always wary of contraband that might be secreted in the girls' "little brown purses." Strict limitations on body searches meant that a visual and a body pat-down by sheriffs were within our rights, but internal orifices could only explored by a physician. I was often called upon for look-sees but no touchies. Seeing evidence of contraband was one thing—groping for it was a no-no!

The odd time contraband descended into the visual field when the prisoner dropped shorts. The sheriff would then order the woman to remove it, seize the contraband and document the incident. The incident could result in the laying of further charges such as possession of an illegal substance or possession of a dangerous weapon. If I clarified what kind of dangerous weapon I've seen and where it was stashed, you would probably never again use a Phillips screwdriver or peel another spud without a phantom pain based on my description.

Handing it over was often stressful for the prisoner, because contraband represented legal tender and safety in the joint. In many cases other inmates would confront a new admission on her arrival in custody to check if she was "packing" contraband of some description. Some of those newly remanded, arrested and subsequently detained for relatively minor offences were merely following instructions by an inmate to act as a "mule" for drug deliveries to the facility.

Certain other forms of possible contraband were obvious: alteration of one's physical attributes in the form of gender and physical modifications—artificial, half-and-half and total. Transvestites were always searched and housed separately from other prisoners to prevent harassment by other prisoners or a problem for the sheriffs. There is a big difference between transvestites and transsexuals in attitude and circumstance.

I'm going to now introduce Belinda and Adele. When these "chicks" came over from the police cells, there was usually a story to tell and a laugh to be had. They shared the same occupation: they were both trannies working on the street. The definition of transvestite is in your Funk and Wagnalls—but in my world it meant their funkies were still waggin'.

Belinda and Adele were seldom in custody at the same time but both of them were very well known to jail staff. Neither was a management problem. Both of them liked to flirt with the new sheriffs.

The two trannies didn't mind speaking openly about their sexual orientation with anyone on cell duty. Once I overheard a conversation between Belinda and one of the veteran sheriffs, who was doing a search in the cell. Belinda told the sheriff that she was scheduled for gender surgery. The sheriff asked, "Are you really going to cut that off?" Belinda replied in the affirmative. The sheriff, who shall remain nameless, expressed his surprise by asking, "Seriously, you are having it cut off?" Belinda replied, "Yes, I have finally made the decision." The sheriff then asked, "Well then, could I have it?" The sheriff's request certainly gave Belinda and all of us a really good laugh to start the day!

The "girls" liked to joke with the new sheriffs just to see them blush. Belinda and Adele loved to say, "Come here, little boy, I've got candy," or "Will you still love me in the morning?" The sheriffs learned quickly to ignore their comments; the novelty wears off when there is no reaction or audience.

Belinda did have the surgery eventually, and arrived happily in our cells with her official documentation. When I made my rounds of the female holding cells she asked me excitedly if I wanted to see her little "muff." I smiled at her and included the documentation as part of her health assessment for the Lakeside Correctional Centre for Women.

When Adele and I met for the first time, "she" was remanded in custody to the Lakeside Correctional Centre for Women. I asked for her gender surgical document but she said did not have it with her. I contacted the police nurse and asked if the paperwork was in her effects or if her altered gender had been confirmed visually at V.P.D. The duty nurse replied that it had been a nightmare for arrests the night before and she wasn't certain. Adele was housed alone in the police cells on arrest and transported to our cells as a person of "undetermined gender."

Well, "undetermined" is not an acceptable entry on my health assessment for a new admission to the Lakeside Correctional Centre. Adele was a bit perturbed when I informed her that it was show-and-tell time.

She complied with the female sheriff's instructions to turn and place her hands on the wall after removing her undies. I had a pretty good rear view of her hiney and it appeared female while her butt cheeks were firmly together. I asked her to put her feet apart, which resulted in a significant "fall-out" of a male appendage. My response at that point was, "Oh my, I won't be sending you to Lakeside with that. Now mind your step as you walk back to the cell."

If this assessment had taken place closer to the end of my twenty-eight years my comment would likely have started with, "Holy shit!" It took a few years in the cells to learn to talk the talk that made my course of action or decision very clear!

Adele and I laughed and joked about it on future visits. The response on one occasion was, "Ah, come on, Bonnie, it's only for one night. I'm being released tomorrow." I laughed, but her night was spent in the male Crowbar Hotel.

It was a sort of initiation to the holding cells to delegate auxiliary deputy sheriffs to search transvestites. The regular sheriffs got a laugh out of the J.A.F.A's reaction and the prisoners' comments. Auxiliary sheriffs were nervous enough on their first shift but they carried out the required searches according to the book. They knew the prisoner's gender status prior to the search but blushing is a difficult reaction to hide.

I should mention that in the old days the regular sheriffs gave the title of J.A.F.A. to auxiliary sheriffs. It took me a while to decipher the code but I made no bones about finding the acronym offensive. The designation is unacceptable now. "Just Another Fucking Auxiliary" does not sit well with employees or management. Such a demoralizing title to give to a competent staff member who stands beside you! Reprimands of serious consequence are in place should anyone use the term now. It was a joke that went very wrong.

Officially Lakeside was the only women's federal correctional institution in the province, although Twin Maples held a few federal prisoners. It was a separate two-storey facility on the same grounds as the Oakalla men's facility. Unlike Oakalla, Lakeside housed inmates held on both federal and provincial statutes.

The women were held in different locations in the institution depending on their custody status. Those serving two years or more were held on the second floor. Those sentenced to two years less a day, and remanded prisoners, were housed on the main floor.

The next closest federal institution for females serving sentences of more than two years was Kingston Penitentiary for Women in Ontario. Very few federally-sentenced females were granted dispensation to serve their time in B.C., on the second floor of the Lakeside Centre. Exceptions were usually related to family illness or child visitation. The prisoner might also be awaiting a decision on another charge in our jurisdiction. Occasionally arrangements were made to house a newborn or toddler with the mother in a special unit, often due to feeding and nurturing requirements.

In some cases, it was a blessing for the expectant mother to be incarcerated for an offence. At the very least, her health and that of her fetus would be monitored and documented. Most importantly, the hospital would be prepared for potential problems on birthing day.

It doesn't take a lot of grey matter to realize that it would be cost-effective to keep a prisoner in the province until all her charges were dealt with. Unfortunately, the Ministry of the Attorney General did not seize the opportunity to save tax pennies in many cases over the years. The decision made by the A.G. was that sheriff escorts were required to escort females the 3,000 miles back and forth until all the charges were dealt with.

Think about it for a second. Two sheriffs fly back and forth to Ontario, both on overtime salary, hotel and meal expenses included, to bring a female back to B.C. to face "boinking" charges! Hello, taxpayer, check your pockets for lint!

Ten:
In and Out of Court

The courts are badly clogged—it takes years for some charges to be adjudicated. If accused people are found guilty, where do we put them? A great number of those charged have mental health issues that cannot be managed by the court or correctional systems.

The Forensic Psychiatric Institution in Coquitlam and the Matsqui Psychiatric Institution have full time mental health staff, but are often at capacity. Other provincial correctional facilities try to house mentally-ill people in a secure area but no in-depth treatment is available there.

The services in these institutions are not readily accessible, so safety becomes an issue for employees in jails or correctional facilities. Institutions do not have the time, staff or ability to handle the frustration level needed to look after people with mental health issues.

I mentioned earlier that Harry and others like him had to be housed and transported separately from other inmates. Marginalized prisoners run a high risk of being injured by other prisoners. Assaults may be triggered by a minor irritation or may just occur for a lark.

Sheriffs often have to deal with this problem during transport because space is limited, and is compounded by the length of travel time required to move inmates back and forth to institutions. A volatile situation can erupt and create an unsafe condition for everyone.

Surprisingly the hardcore con was generally protective toward a prisoner displaying mental health problems if transported in a common vehicle. It was the younger "weekend warrior" who thought it was fun to hassle the vulnerable—it made the trip more entertaining for them.

It wasn't uncommon for the old-timers to provide a little discipline of their own to settle a situation. They disliked the smartass "new fish," who tended to try their patience and interrupt their naps on long van rides. This method of intervention was fine with the escorts, because it is unsafe and against policy for the escort vehicle to be opened for sheriffs to intervene en route. And you could count on the inmates' Code of Silence—know nothing, hear nothing, see nothing.

I not only trained all of the staff as first responders, I provided seizure assessment and management services in all areas of the courthouse. Withdrawal associated with heavy alcohol and drug abuse was a daily nursing challenge, especially if the prisoner involved was making a first-time appearance on the police load. It was usually the result of acute intoxication and could evolve into a life-threatening situation. Symptoms of overdose or withdrawal can manifest themselves after some delay, leading to rapid deterioration, aspiration of vomit or seizures. If seizures occur, there is also the danger of secondary trauma depending on the type of seizure and its intensity. Staff members acted as first responders and I was called right away when seizures occurred.

Anyone in the cells thought to be under the influence of a substance was given a "shake and shout" at regular intervals by the sheriffs, the results of which were documented on a check sheet at my request. I relied on the first responder training and experience of the deputy sheriffs to give me the heads up if we needed to assess a prisoner's state further.

What, when, how and how long—these were key questions I asked myself throughout my hands-on health assessments in such situations. I asked sheriffs and prisoners if they had witnessed anything. People usually gave me a complete description of the event if they saw it. In many of these emergency incidents the patient would be confused or combative, or exhibited a marked reduction in L.O.C. (level of consciousness) so I could not question them directly.

I was assisted by a sheriff who monitored the pulse while another called 911. My duty was to document what I found when assessing the prisoner's vital signs and to prepare a history of my findings to give to Emergency Services on their arrival. I documented all of this information at the patient's side, passing the information on to the sheriff supervisor, who then informed the prosecutor and defence lawyer.

It was not that my ability was in question; it was a matter of court record. In cases like these, the courts had to put over the charged person until he or she was seen by a physician because of a documented inability to understand or instruct counsel. If the circumstances were of a sufficiently serious nature for the courts to put the person over, he required immediate hospital transfer by ambulance. Only a life-threatening state that would compromise the prisoner's health further is an acceptable reason for non-appearance in court. Aside from that, in they go. It is most important not to cause an unnecessary delay of proceedings that could result in a dismissal or stay of the charges.

Sometimes prisoners tried to use sickness to avoid appearing due to the nature of their charges or because they planned to escape from the hospital. Others were tired of sitting in cells all day and wanted an early return to their institutions after their court appearances, or prompt release.

Defence lawyers sometimes felt that a particular judge slated to hear the charge was known to come down hard on certain offences. The lawyer's intention was likely to ask that the case be put over for appearance before a judge with a history of being more lenient. One lawyer appeared to make a habit of delaying court proceedings on charges. He could have been one of those who inspired jokes about lawyers.

In contrast, many extremely reputable lawyers had an eye on court, taxpayer and witness costs. They would see to it that a less urgent or serious charge would be dealt with promptly so the entire volume of cases moved through the crowded court system in a reasonable time period.

The correctional facility received all the health information for people remanded in custody. I often advised or referred people being released on charges to attend a treatment clinic for investigation into their health complaints.

Mental health issues and lucidity can also interfere with court procedure. *Compos mentis* is a Latin term that addresses a person's ability to understand a charge and communicate effectively with his or her legal representative. The person charged must be able to instruct a lawyer. They must be able to comprehend the nature of the charge and the decision of the court.

I generally determined, along with input from the court mental health worker, whether the accused was lucid and could comprehend the proceedings. If we found culpable mental health interference was present that would compromise the court appearance, the accused would be remanded in custody until a qualified physician could do a complete assessment of physical and psychological status. The documentation would subsequently be made available to the court.

If the prisoner had a history of mental health problems and a fear of being detained in custody he often required Mental Patients Association (M.P.A.) support. The prisoner was reassured when the M.P.A. court worker attended the court appearance. It also provided an opportunity for intervention if the court gave the prisoner a release order.

It may still be the case today, but while I was there a multifaceted system of community services was available within the courthouse to support an individual's court appearance. Salvation Army court representatives, Mental Patients' Association court counsellors and Native court workers all cooperated for the benefit of all the people in the courthouse each day. Everyone focused on the best interests of the accused along with the safety implications of his or her possible release. It took a concerted daily effort by the affiliated court services to arrange secure housing, food, clothing and supportive counselling in the community to meet a client's physical or mental needs. The attendance requirement in fact sometimes formed part of a release decision. In these cases, the judge might order that the person be released to a service agency court worker who assisted the person in gaining access to the appropriate community services, such as housing, mental health services or detox.

Many people in custody have not accessed services in the community prior to their arrest. They slip through the cracks into our legal system. Charges are often a secondary result of a primary problem that has not been addressed by the appropriate community service agency.

I want to give credit where credit is due. Victims' Services, M.P.A. and the Sally Ann were (and are) unsung heroes who provide comfort, support and occasional childcare while the child's primary care provider is in the courtroom. Whether it's clothing, pet care arrangements, plugging a parking meter, a bus or meal ticket, referral follow-up or transportation to a care facility, First Nations workers and mental health co-ordinators are vital resources on site in the courthouse.

Giving comfort to families is an important task, but heartrending for the workers. Victims' families are not always given time in court to speak about their feelings of loss. Prior to sentencing, a convicted person seldom hears of the pain the family has suffered because of his offence. Family members have fewer rights than the accused and the convicted. The sentencing decision is often put over for a period of time to consider an appropriate sentence for the convicted, which prolongs the agony.

An expression of loss by a family member is a facet of the conviction that should be documented as such. The decision has been made—the guilt has been confirmed—so allow the words to be heard as a victim's right. It is a part of the grieving process to be able to express feelings of anger, loss and deprivation for a child or parenting partner, or for financial and emotional support. Supreme Court judges often allow victim and family comments but generally victims, families and friends sit without speaking in provincial courts. A judge may or may not take their words into consideration for sentencing but the words should be said and heard, not left festering in unspoken grief.

White-collar criminals are often given time at institutions like the now-closed Ferndale "Golf and Country Club," or may serve only on weekends at the former New Haven on Marine Drive Even the occasional capital offender ends up in minimum security, whether transferred there in error or as a result of pulled strings. Housing the convicted in a minimum security facility, where they can play golf without any greens fees, is in my opinion an inappropriate sentence. It is difficult for victims left in the wake of an offence to accept. Lady Justice is peeking from under her blindfold in select cases, methinks.

Sometimes, money or the societal level of the convicted play a significant role in a sentencing decision. It was very difficult in some cases to remain impartial as demanded by our employee protocol.

I never saw sheriffs abuse the protocol of impartiality in any way, but I have also never seen anyone get a hug when they left our cells. The sheriffs and I did, in fact, privately counsel certain prisoners to consider protective custody for their own safety. I have also shed my own private tears for victims and their families over the years. I usually addressed the emotion while driving home after work so I could leave it at work. The hour's drive allowed me time to re-focus and not take my anxiety home with me. I often pulled into Rocky Point Park in Port Moody to reflect on the events of the day: perhaps a horrendous criminal offence involving children, the sudden demise of a client I had known for many years or particularly stressful events during my shift. I was a mother, wife and human being: roles to be enjoyed, anticipated and remembered as separate from the anxieties and stress of my work.

Eleven:
Becoming
Politically Correct

Human rights legislation in the mid-'80s clearly defined the ways Canada addressed sensitive issues relating to culture, sexuality and race. Public discussion of information such as names or characteristics that could identify someone or their charges was specified as contrary to the sheriffs' departmental policy of impartiality. The rule was that sheriffs, along with any other staff member in the court system, had to detach themselves from any personal discussions to maintain a prisoner's safety and right to an unbiased hearing. This made it tough on the odd occasion if they were asking for "Skinner" to come out of a cell that held thirty-five prisoners... an unfortunate last name in a jailhouse setting. The other name that got more than one verbal response happened when the sheriff was calling out a prisoner to see his lawyer. He approached Cell #5 and said, "Crook, your lawyer's here." Quite a few crooks moved toward the gate, laughing.

It is not my intention to make light of the discrimination requirement. The names mentioned are just examples of innocent but real funnies stemming from the protocols. In truth, maintaining such a policy of confidentiality was considered to be of prime importance to ensure prisoner safety and staff security.

Initially there seemed to be a bit of overkill in putting the necessary changes into effect. Even *National Geographic* magazines were banned in the holding cells for all staff and inmates because the pictures of half-naked males or females were considered unacceptable. On the face of it, it seemed silly. If we allowed something like *National Geographic* to offend us then how could we handle the realities of serious crime on a daily basis or the sexual slurs from a packed cell of horny inmates serving lengthy sentences?

Playboy magazines became definite contraband, even though you and I both know that the only items of interest for gentlemen were the articles. I imagine staff members may have taken some home, strictly for educational purposes, you understand. A picture is worth a thousand words.

At the same time, all calendars depicting naked women, and posters or memorabilia from No. 5 Orange had to be removed from the walls of the records office. The amusing thing about being asked to remove these particular works of art was that the only people who used the office on a daily basis were the senior records sheriff (female) and me. I can honestly say that neither of us was interested in the wall décor and neither of us was offended. In fact, think I recall labelling each part of one of the pictures with the correct anatomical terminology. We were the butt of jokes now and then when other staff members entered the office and saw us surrounded by naked chicks on the walls. The pictures were promptly removed without question. I did consider putting up a black velvet painting of the King of Rock and Roll to replace them—fully clothed, of course.

As a side note, none of the raunchy pictures discussed above were ever visible to inmates but raunchy pictures were often found in prisoners' effects on their arrival. These items went with the person on remand, sentence or release, bagged as personal property.

In the long run, the Human Rights Act was a sound decision by our lawmakers. Our changing society demanded the law pass without question, exemption or delay.

Twelve:
Crossing the Street

A six-storey remand centre was built in 1985 where I'd previously parked my car. A tunnel connected it to the provincial courts and it was designated as a maximum security state of the art facility. It underwent extensive renovations in 1998 and our own court holding cells were renovated twice within five years.

This multimillion-dollar facility closed its doors in 2001. It was obsolete as soon as it opened: inmates were double-bunking in a short time and later prisoners had to sleep in the gym because of the overcrowding. The only prisoners held in this facility after its closure to the general population were the charged Air India bombers. It closed tight when the trial concluded, after about a year.

The final straw for me was also in 1998, when the province came up with a pie-in-the-sky idea to combine the V.P.D., the court holding cells and the pre-trial centre. The court cells were to become a twenty-four-hour-a-day facility for V.P.D. and Corrections. The sheriffs were renamed Sheriff Court Services staff and the sheriff escorts were relocated to the Riverview grounds in Coquitlam, midway between downtown and the Fraser Valley institutions.

Astute, knowledgeable observation and intervention strategies are major requirements for staff members of any holding facility. We anticipated confusion and miscommunication around the arrested, charged and convicted after the amalgamation of the three facilities, which resulted in very unhappy, frustrated staff.

Before the change, the nurses from the police cells and the pre-trial health unit were on pins and needles. They were almost the last to know what was going to happen to their jobs. Me, I was not anxious. I'd served my time. I did not want any part of that doomed-to-failure plan. I thought, and still think, it was a bunch of illogical bullshit decisions compounded by the loss of an enormous amount of taxpayers' dollars. This is no hearsay: I saw, I heard. I had also been the B.C. Nurses' Union and the Registered Psychiatric Nurses' Union (R.P.N.U.) nursing steward for fifteen years. Ta-ta for now to Sheriff Court Services and the new Vancouver Pre-trial Services Centre! I was out of there, retiring on February 5, 1999.

But I didn't really retire—taking up knitting wasn't my style. I headed directly across Main Street to D.E.Y.A.S., the Downtown Eastside Youth Activities Services Society. I'd been covering shifts on their mobile health van since 1998 in my off-duty hours, and now I would do the work full time.

I had tears in my eyes on turning a life page and optimism in my heart that a plan to streamline the D.E.Y.A.S. health outreach van program would become a reality. I felt needed in a different capacity: needed to provide a unique service to the forgotten society and to people I had known for so many years in Vancouver's Downtown Eastside.

Me and my colleagues at my retirement from the courthouse,
February 1999.

Thirteen:
Pay What Justice Costs

Officers involved in the criminal justice system in B.C. are being shrugged off and systematically shortchanged (pun intended). The point could be made federally as well with the R.C.M.P. and customs and immigration officers. All three levels of government are involved in grossly discriminatory salary abuse without taking a serious look at the job description of each position and the potential dangers involved.

The budget for security in every area of prisoner management—police, sheriffs and correctional officers—is insufficient to deal with the degree of potential violence facing these professionals. The budget for health and hospital nursing professionals ranks right up (or maybe I should say down) there as well. Violence is a smouldering, dormant possibility for all these workers, something that could erupt into reality in the blink of an eye.

The men and women who wear the uniform of the Vancouver city police work alongside some of the most well-trained justice officers in Canada. V.P.D. salaries, benefits and pension plans are among the best for all Canadian police forces. Officers work four eleven-hour shifts followed by four days off. The V.P.D. gross yearly salary scale (as of January 2008) is broken down by years of service as follows:

Probationary Constable	$52,233.00
4th Class Constable (one year's service)	$55,964.00
3rd Class Constable (two years' service)	$59,695.00
2nd Class Constable (three years' service)	$67,157.00
1st Class Constable (four years' service)	$74,619.00
After ten years' service	$78,350.00
After fifteen years' service	$82,081.00
After twenty years' service	$85,812.00

In contrast, deputy sheriff salaries as of April 7, 2008 were $28,000.00 less annually than any other peace officer. They are the lowest-paid law enforcement personnel in B.C. Because other law enforcement agencies pay up to forty percent more, staff shortages have an impact on the operation of B.C.'s courts, its prisoner management and prisoner transport. Sheriffs work at 440 courts and transport facilities across the province, and in 2007, fifty-seven deputies left the B.C. Sheriff Service. As of April 2008, the B.C. Government Employees' Union (B.C.G.E.U.) reported that more than fourteen left the service. The Campbell government rebuffed any attempt to negotiate special pay adjustments to solve shortages and to deal with significant recruitment and retention pressures. Take a look at these hourly rate comparisons.

- Translink transit police officers: $10.27 per hour (39%) more than sheriffs;
- Vancouver City Police 1st class constables with four years' service: $9.57 (36%) more;
- R.C.M.P. constables with three years' service: $8.36 (32%) more;
- Special provincial constables (unarmed) providing basic legislative security in Victoria: sixty cents more an hour.

If translated to annual salaries, the disparity becomes even more obvious.

- Greater Vancouver transit officers: $28,000 more annually;
- Saanich police constables: $24,549 more annually;
- Delta police constables: $21,700 more annually;
- Federal corrections officers: $22,000 more annually.

Similar studies exist comparing pay rates for B.C. correctional officers, who are paid substantially less than their counterparts in other jurisdictions. In Alberta, deputy sheriffs earned $31.52 per hour in 2008, twenty percent more than in B.C. The only obvious difference between the duties of Alberta sheriffs and B.C. sheriffs is that Alberta sheriffs are also trained to handle traffic violations, thus relieving police officers to attend to other criminal acts endemic in our benevolent Canadian society.

The disparity in wages is abhorrent and totally irresponsible. B.C. deputy sheriffs are armed. They transport prisoners from correctional facilities to courts, and maintain safety and security in provincial and Supreme Court courtrooms across the province. And when I say they transport prisoners, I am not being "Billy Booster" here. I am talking about transporting and securing some of the most dangerous prisoners in B.C., Canada and the world. I know because I was there and I saw them. Clifford Olsen, Robert Noyes, Bindy Johal, Robert Pickton—familiar names, I'm sure. They are but a very few of the high-risk people managed and transported by deputy sheriffs within the province and Canada-wide.

The Justice Institute of B.C. trains male and female deputy sheriffs as accredited peace officers. Sheriffs must maintain great physical fitness, sound tactical intelligence and non-judgmental communication skills, focusing on the safe management of prisoners and others attending a court facility. Sheriffs must also qualify annually in the handling and firing of nine-millimetre automatic weapons. Range training standards are stringent for all shooting positions.

The unknown is always present during a sheriff's work hours just as it is for police officers. There have been numerous bomb threats in courthouses over the years. Sheriffs in the court holding cells must always be aware of their surroundings, and trust their gut feelings. Many times over the twenty-eight years I spent as Sheriff Nurse, people received an unexpected remand or sentence in court and came through the docket like crazed, charging bulls. We did not always know what happened to the charged person in the courtroom. The holding cells stood on guard for thee and me on many occasions!

I might also add that sidearms are not worn in the holding cells, for obvious reasons. Sheriffs are armed with batons and pepper spray, and follow a special cell extraction protocol if necessary. In my day I handed out more than a few cartons of Girl Guide cookies to sheriffs and prisoners who were able to use verbal communication to defuse tense situations.

I personally never felt unsafe or threatened by prisoners' behaviour—I did as I was told, and so did the prisoner in most cases. Teamwork was, and I'm sure still is, paramount in providing safety and respect for all.

Incidentally, in 2010 the B.C.G.E.U. negotiated a spiffy new contract for the sheriffs... which gave them a zero percent increase in both salary and benefits. Hello, what is wrong with this picture, all three levels of government? Hello, taxpayers who are now in the know about despicable wage disparity!

Fourteen:
Blend Services,
Not Lattes

There was, and still is, a great need for multifaceted services in our society. I mentioned people like Harry, Belinda, Adele and others to make readers aware of the reality of the problem. These people are victims of a society that lacks services for very needy, lonely people who then end up in the wrong "pocket" of the provincial budget.

People suffering from mental illness often battle drug addiction as well, making it even more difficult to provide them with appropriate help. They require intervention under Health Services, not the Attorney General's Department. Charging someone does not address the primary problem, and sometimes not even the secondary one. People at this level of society generally do not take their prescribed medication regularly and do not accept agency follow-up in the community. Just like Harry, charges laid against them are often related to mischief and the person is usually released in a short period, becoming a revolving door nuisance. There is no "correction" in Corrections for the marginalized or dual-diagnosis prisoner. There is no staffing or time for it.

The government uses what I believe to be "salesman bafflegab" to blind the voter instead of addressing facts gained from the people who know. Harry and others like him fall through the cracks, ending up in inappropriate places that lack the knowledge and resources to resolve their complicated issues.

Untreated, mentally compromised clients may begin with mischief, but as their disease progresses the response to it escalates to more serious crimes. They are often arrested for dangerous offences that affect society in general. How many fires have to be started or lives jeopardized before we fund treatment of their primary illness appropriately?

We at the courthouse were family to Harry and others. We addressed their need to belong and be cared about. Don't we all have that need? It is a primary need of all human beings. Why is there no safe housing where they can receive psychiatric care and become re-stabilized on appropriate, prescribed medication under the supervision of qualified professionals?

The closing of most of the Riverview Psychiatric Hospital facility between 1984 and 2007 put hundreds of these souls out on the street. The government set up only minimal support systems for these marginalized people, on an insufficient budget unable to handle all the complex issues that faced the ex-patients every day.

Many of those released were reluctant participants in available mental health programs or made use of them ineffectively. They elected to reside in the downtown core, where they felt they would be accepted and where they would not stand out in a crowd. It is very difficult to track people when they become "invisible" in a geographic area. Such marginalized citizens usually have some disability income that makes them prime targets for assaults and robberies. They represent big bucks for drug dealers, and are easy targets for misplaced care and supervision funding.

Once, while I was working for D.E.YA.S., a police officer parked his motorcycle for an hour and handed out jay-walking tickets to women who crossed Hastings to visit our Health Van. They were given another one when they jay-walked back. It happened! I was there and I could not believe it! The government coffers will never see the dollars but the women could land in our overcrowded justice system because of outstanding warrants for unpaid fines. Whoopee! What great "collars" for the cop and what great wallpaper for the women's Skid Row dives, courtesy of the taxpayer. Meanwhile, if there is an arsonist on the rampage in trendy Kitsilano or a tragic incident in Point Grey's upper middle class area, that's a problem that could benefit from officer assistance.

The V.P.D. "Odd Squad" foot patrol was started by police officer Al Arsenault. They were and still are a real asset to harm reduction and intervention efforts in the D.T.E.S.

It is so sad to see these people in jail cells. It is also a police management problem: a burden on officers whose efforts could be used more efficiently somewhere else. Inadequate numbers of police officers have to deal with problems involving compromised people. Officers are called upon to charge these people with various misdemeanours such as mischief, loitering or being a "nuisance". For God's sake put the officer in an area where action results in prevention, intervention and protection.

Robbing Peter to save Paul resolves nothing, but that is what the government has done over the years and continues to do to this very day. There is very little distinction between party mandates in this area. It's a long worn-out path that has been followed by every government with minimal results. Now funds required for the mentally disadvantaged have only been moved to another "pocket" by our current government leaders—from the Health Ministry to Court Services and Corrections.

I have never seen appropriate ongoing supervision of clients displaced from Riverview or other mental health facilities. How can supervision be possible when there is a gross shortage of experienced professional people working in the field of forensic mental health? Professional staff employed in community service who attempt to counsel the "forgotten" feel the domino effect of frustration and disappointment when continuity of access to treatment is interrupted.

The clients and those who are trained and trusted to care for them are all in disadvantaged positions. Too much stress is placed on the police, courts, Corrections and society in general to address mental health problems. There is at present virtually no area in greater Vancouver that has not been affected by dual-diagnosis marginalized people arriving in their living "space." The vulnerable are not just in the D.T.E.S. and shooing them away from the outside cafés so you can drink your lattés in peace isn't working either. Because transit is a piece of cake the need has spread everywhere.

Government needs to recognize that there is no "correction" in Corrections for the marginalized offender. Incarceration merely postpones a chronic problem. Until the proper housing facilities and a staff of mental health professionals are in place to help the most vulnerable members of our society, problems will continue both for Corrections and for society, anywhere and anytime.

The city of Vancouver and the Lower Mainland are havens for gangland activities, but there is no geographical area in the province where violence is not likely to occur. Nor is there a "dark of night"—any one of us could be caught in the middle of a potentially harmful situation at any time. A recent example is the stabbing and decapitation of a sleeping young man on a Greyhound bus. We do not live in Never Never Land. This is a reality check for all of us. Interestingly, in the situation I mentioned, the R.C.M.P. spent over an hour trying to talk the killer into dropping his weapon. Only a few months before, a disturbed and unarmed immigrant had been tasered by the R.C.M.P. at the Vancouver International Airport just a short time after arrival, and died as a result. The man at the airport was not waving a decapitated head as a trophy, while the one on the bus was attempting to do exactly that.

Sheriffs are specially selected and trained to manage not only high profile prisoners—mass murderers and well-known gang members—but also the prisoners' compatriots in the gallery, a victims' family and friends and any Joe Citizen who might be in court.

Wally Oppal was named B.C. Attorney General in 2005 after a distinguished career as a judge in the Canadian Supreme Court. He saw firsthand the professionalism and dedication of sheriffs during his twenty-five years on the bench.

I heard him speaking about the jury's second-degree murder conviction of Robert Pickton. Wally Oppal made special comments about the respectful and focused duties of the sheriffs, who were selected for competence and trained for consistency and safety in all areas for the pre-trial *voir dire* and the trial itself. It was a very traumatic trial for everyone—families, friends, news media and others listening to the circumstances and seeing the evidence.

The team of sheriffs involved were dedicated to ensuring that the security of the New Westminster Supreme Court was beyond reproach. These men and women were specially trained in defensive driving, intervention and searches. Everyone entering the facility was subject to detailed, regular monitoring.

The team showed great respect to the families of the victims. They allocated a pass-controlled media access room in which a sheriff was present at all times. The sheriffs also kept the media's TV cameras and interviews from harassing people on the outside plaza of the courthouse. I was present when a sheriff instructed the media that they were to remain behind the barricade separating the public from the court-controlled area of the plaza designated for victims' families and others involved in the trial. A short time later the same sheriff left the courthouse to request the barricades be returned to their original positions. The paparazzi had moved the gates closer but *were* technically still behind them.

Since being named Attorney General in 2005, Wally Oppal has faced new realities in security and law enforcement, especially during the Pickton trial. As a Supreme Court judge he became familiar with sheriffs' professional management of dangerous prisoners in court settings.

He was quoted in the *Surrey Now* on August 21, 2007, "… they are extremely well-trained people and I have no doubt they could perform other duties to assist the police… Maybe we could free (the police) up and have sheriffs assist them, but we have to discuss these things with the police… You have to be careful to not do anything improper that would be contrary to any collective agreement."

The collective agreement is a non-issue, Mr. Oppal. Semantics should never play a role in policing and public safety. The real problem is that the sheriffs are under the B.C.G.E.U. as the only union members who carry firearms—all the other B.C.G.E.U. members only carry pencils!—when they should be part of the police union. It is up to the city of Vancouver and the Ministry of the Attorney General to place deputy sheriffs under a police service addendum similar to Alberta's sheriffs. This would allow them to assume duties that free up police officers for serious crime prevention and intervention.

Addendum September 28, 2010: The provincial government announced the appointment of former judge and Attorney General Wally Oppal to head a public inquiry relating to policing delays and the "Missing Women" case. It was greeted with enthusiasm by the families of the missing women, and current A.G. Michael de Jong commented that Mr. Oppal "has an impeccable track record of public service." I agree!

Fifteen:
Prioritize Justice

The forgotten person is the victim of an offence or a family member who sits in the gallery of the courtroom; listens to the details of the offence and cries following the court decision. The tears are often the result of the punishment not fitting the crime. Canada's justice system has not addressed or altered the punishment for crimes that are a reality in the 21st century. This country has always been about ten years behind the United States, with too many concurrent sentences for major crimes. Life should mean life, not twenty-five years without parole.

It must be very demoralizing to police officers and prosecutors when a perp hits the street before their own shifts have ended. It sure pissed me off one day when a notorious gang leader came out of court smiling. He was released on bail, the very large amount of cash having been paid by a gang member. He was out within an hour! However, what goes around really does come around—he was shot dead by a rival gang while dancing in a downtown club.

In my career, I also have seen many lifers on the street after serving about half their sentences. In Canada good behaviour and time in custody awaiting trial reduces the sentence, but it does not reduce the grief of a victim's family. I believe that horrendous crimes against people should not be rewarded.

Get a grip and just maybe the offenders will see things in a different light. Put an atta-boy star on the calendar, but remember—the con has pooped on our Cheerios, so let him earn cookies in jail without decreasing the sentence. Society can do without him tossing his cookies in an alley for us to clean up, or raping another woman! Corrections calls it early release for good behaviour. Excuse me, but what happened to the bad behaviour that put him in there?

Eleven murder convictions result in eleven consecutive life sentences in the U.S.A. The death penalty is still on the books in Washington State, Florida, Texas and others.

I would like to see a referendum on sentencing for murders of children and officers in the line of duty. I also want a say in the convicted receiving university degrees at our expense. Our kids work twenty years or more to pay off student loans and I know, firsthand, of women working the streets to pay their way through university. Whaaateeeverrr!

Part Two:
Drugged

Sixteen:
Getting Started

I experienced a smidgen of anxiety walking through the front door of the D.E.Y.A.S. office on February 8, 1999, excusing myself past a line-up of clients waiting to exchange needles, use the phone or a meet a counselling appointment. There were so many familiar faces from my life on the other side of the street!

Some of them gave me bewildered looks and some announced, "You're the nurse from the holding cells." I thought of replying, "No, that's my twin," while I tried to recall whether I had refused them a Jolly Rancher while in custody. The blue jeans, hiking boots, scarf and jacket could not disguise the snow-white hair that had glowed in the dark of the holding cells.

It was 1:30 PM on a Monday. Silent curiosity about my attire and presence could be cut with a knife until a tall First Nations D.E.Y.A.S. employee grinned at me and asked in a loud voice, "Since when did we start hiring old ladies in here?"

He then introduced me to a senior male drug counsellor—"Hey, Grampaw, meet Granmaw!" I smiled at him and reminded him to never turn your back on a nurse. A voice echoed from a client waiting, "Yeah, especially that nurse!"

It was my first day on my clients' turf, leading to a night of eye-opening surprises and learning experiences for a tough old broad. I felt a bit apprehensive but challenged, especially when I learned that my driver for the shift would be "Smudge"—the same person who announced my arrival and did the introductions.

I underwent a routine orientation, the usual obligatory paper signing, photo ID and a big welcome from John Turvey, executive director and a respected friend for many years.

The photo ID was—not surprising to me—a comedy of photo background problems due to my hair colour. Several unsuccessful snaps were taken before I visibly had hair. The trashcan photos showed a face with no head or hair outlines: a Cheshire cat out of *Alice in Wonderland*! I felt like I was in wonderland enough without the picture evidence. My ID as "Nurse, D.E.Y.A.S. Health Outreach Van" finally resulted in a plastic clip card with hard-earned white-hair iridescent me, in living colour.

My driver and I headed off in the clinic on wheels for a drive-by of the regular designated stops and the general geographic areas we covered downtown back in 1999: north to the waterfront, south to 41st Avenue, west to English Bay and east to Boundary Road, with lots of zigs and zags in all directions—through alleys, around schools, past housing projects and parks.

Overwhelming changes were in store for the Health Van, unbeknownst to us. It became a "you-ain't-seen-nothing-yet" evolution in one short year as we changed and expanded the program to include more geographic areas and more family contact. We also had to deal with significant changes in the kinds of drugs on the street, and their effects.

Seventeen:
Manny and Me and the Health Van Makes Three

My full-time driver, Manny Cu, took the wheel of the Health Van on my second day at D.E.Y.A.S., and remained my driver for the entire time I was there. Manny had been in recovery for about eight years when I met him. He'd been born in the Philippines; his mom is Filipino and his father Asian. Although his full name is Vincenzo Emmanuel Cu, he always used his middle name and went by Manny.

I asked, "Why don't you use your first name?"

"Because Vinny is a crook name."

"Oh, and Manny isn't?"

Ya think?

Manny and I always arrived at the office an hour before our shift, about 1:30 PM. We were the full-time Health Van staff and relief days were covered by an auxiliary nurse and another van driver who Manny had oriented to the work we did. We had to package medication, order supplies and restock the clinic area of the van. The time also allowed us to connect and enjoy the camaraderie with other employees whose hours did not coincide with ours.

We spent part of the hour following up on messages left for the Health Van. Sometimes there would be a visit request by the physician at the Downtown Health Clinic (D.T.H.C.) to check on a client or do dressing changes after hours, asking us to report our findings by a return phone call or e-mail message to D.T.H.C. Most days we also got requests to pick up packaged medication to be delivered to D.T.H.C. patients at their residences. I would administer the medication after assessing the client's blood pressure, pulse and temperature, and checking mental and cognitive function. I sometimes withheld medication based on my findings (if the patient had a history of not complying with doctors' orders) and occasionally the client needed referral to a hospital for intervention.

We put stock medication in small sealed envelopes in maximum amounts of six pills, labelled with contents and dosage instructions: Tylenol, lozenges, Advil, laxatives and vitamins. Other preparations, such as Epsom salts, antiseptic hand soap and liquid Maalox, were put in appropriate two-ounce medication containers from bulk supply at the office, then labelled for client use.

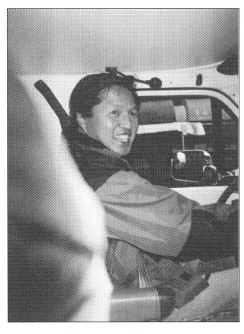

"Mannykins" could be stubborn like most men are at times, recovered addicts especially! "Nope, I don't take any pills, alcohol or smoke... I'll be fine." he would say.

Manny on the van.

He was feeling crappy with cold symptoms one evening. I noticed he was wheezy and finally he agreed to go to Downtown Native Health Services in the 400 block of East Main Street. It was open until 8 PM with a doctor available. I waited while the female physician took him in to the examining room. It was a long wait for a simple check of the neck and chest—I knew Manny would be pissed off about the patient history he would likely be asked to provide.

I sat there smiling while I waited—I'm a nurse. I knew! When he emerged from the room, the look on his face told me the question had been asked.

"When was your prostate last checked?"

"Never," replied Manny.

Well, it certainly was checked on that visit. He was also given a Ventolin inhaler for the other end. Upon leaving the clinic, he asked the doctor if she would still love him tomorrow, but she was very professional and did not react to his comment with anything other than "good-bye."

I laughed so hard I nearly busted a gut, and began to sing a mouldy oldie: "Will you still love me tomorrow…" once we got in the van. I believe he made his traditional comment, "Come closer so I can slap you." To this day he likely thinks I knew that an examination of his nether regions might be done; after all, I was a nurse. Sure, I was a nurse, but we certainly never discussed his "boys" at any time! And if I had so much as hinted that it might happen he would never have gone to the clinic in the first place.

Singing was always fun while driving. We were the Sonny and Cher of the Downtown Eastside (D.T.E.S). We did Johnny Cash and Roy Orbison, and Elvis was a favourite: "Heartbreak Hotel," "Jailhouse Rock," "Are You Lonesome Tonight." One of us would start singing and the other would have to sing the next line.

Another pastime while driving was to see who could come up with the most words beginning with the letter D that described the weather and the areas we frequented. Why only that particular letter, I don't know. Manny started it on one of his dorky days, I guess. Dank, dark, dismal, dreaded, dingy—others too, which I determined to be "erudite neologisms." I love it when I say something that requires research to define!

One of the regular scheduled van stops (especially in summer, when the city saw an influx of transients) was Cathedral Park across from Christ Church, in the city centre. We parked in the adjacent lane, where the van driver exchanged used "rigs" (syringes and needles) for new ones along with swabs, sterile water and conversation. The driver, as an addict in recovery for several years, was a necessary part of rounding out the Health Van's credibility. He or she provided the client with education, support, encouragement and a role model: proof that their glass was half-full, not half-empty. Many of the clients around the small park were transient youth new to Vancouver and unfamiliar to services

available in the city.

I handled the clinical and health issues of the clients, not all of whom were addicted but required intervention for wounds, physiological information or referral to a physician. More often, over time, I was a "Mom" person who gave them a Tylenol, a band-aid or a hug—*prn.*

The stops, along with St. Paul's Hospital visits twice weekly, took place between 2:30 PM and 5:30 PM daily, followed by a stop at the office to take care of our elimination requirements. The hours from 6:30 PM to 9:00 PM held the potential for floating eyeballs without the throne-room stop, trust me! We were there in the centre of it, from the W.I.S.H. stop at 6:30 PM, buzzing all over the city like flies on a lawn torpedo until our supper break at 9.

Once we were actually detoured back to the office following an emergency call to Powell Place, a safe place for women and children. Manny and I made a rush call to do a health assessment on a young child running a high fever. We parked outside the facility; I grabbed my stethoscope, thermo-scan and other equipment and Manny buzzed for entry.

We were there for about a half-hour seeing several other clients along with the little guy, who was about two years old. He had some snuffles and dry, warm skin but was sure aware that I was there. I gave the staff member some infant Tylenol to administer and asked his mom to give him a tepid bath followed by a good cuddle.

A part of my childcare treatment assessment was to blow up disposable gloves and draw faces on them—it eased anxiety for the kids and me. I liked to fill one up with water in the bathtub and prick a hole in one of the fingers—a neat squirt gun in the tub and a bit of mopping for a wet mom afterwards. It usually worked, along with a nice cold Freezie or a Popsicle, to occupy a youngster's attention while I checked them over like Miss Piggy assisted by Manny as Kermit the Frog.

We left Powell Place. When we returned to the van I felt a squishy sensation under my foot as I opened the passenger door—an unexpected delivery of fresh bowel evacuation to the deep treads of my boot. The abominable (or is it abdominal?) gift had not been there when I exited the van on our arrival. I had the feeling that I had done a little more than piss off a client that night.

Manny gave me immediate intervention instructions. I was to remove my hiking boot and hang it out of the window while we drove back to the office for a retread. I thought that was bullshit but I did as instructed. I am a nurse; I wasn't angry. We only get excited about bowel function when properly executed and documented.

The van also made routine home visits to deliver meals from the Evelyn Saller Centre cafeteria on Alexander Street to housebound clients who were ill, elderly or otherwise disabled. The hot meal was paid for with meal tickets purchased by several non-profit societies as well as D.E.Y.A.S. The nominal cost was $1.50 and was much appreciated by many who did not have cash. These were used for positive intervention and not handed out haphazardly. The same applied to local transit tickets. We would never use them to enable unacceptable intentions such as to go and "boost" at a shopping mall or to sell drugs in the garden smoking area off the third floor of St. Paul's Hospital. We wrote up information on what was given out to whom every shift along with client stats, for consistency among D.E.Y.A.S. staff.

Many elderly citizens in the Downtown Eastside live in deplorably rat- and vermin-infested housing. These people are law-abiding citizens who reside there due to circumstance and need. Personal safety is a very real concern to them. They are in danger of becoming victims anytime they step out the door. Many older citizens watched for the Health Van to make its regular stop and would wait in line for a visit, vitamins or the annual flu vaccine. A safe, friendly place to talk is good medicine for very lonely souls who do not ask for much: just a hug and a chat with people who care enough to remember their names. It was important for my driver and me to spend time with them and see them smile or thank us for the "room service" we provided, bringing them food during inclement weather.

Manny and I picked up a meal and medication for one particular gentleman and delivered them daily at the beginning of our shift. Bobby was a special person we had known for many years and the early stop allowed time for a friendly sit-down visit. The visits ended suddenly when we were told of his death when we arrived at work one day. We walked over to the Brandiz Hotel to look for any next-of-kin information in his room and found a note with an Alberta number on it. I phoned it, and got a cousin who wasn't much interested. While walking back to the D.E.Y.A.S. office, I mentioned that I truly felt heartache at the loss of our Bobby.

The aching continued through the several hours of our shift. We were catching up on some paperwork, and Manny was on the computer with his back to me while I worked at the desk. One of the street nurses came down to use the photocopier and saw me sweating and short of breath. Manny was p.o'd and said, "You're really having pain. Why didn't you say something?" Alarmed, he called Emergency Services to check me out. It was a unique experience to be hooked up to oxygen and an E.C.G. and loaded into an ambulance on a gurney while a client asked me for a lozenge!

Manny came to St. Paul's Hospital with me. When I was stable and on a gurney in the hospital hallway waiting for the test results my daughter arrived. Unbeknownst to me he had called her to meet us there. When she got there he told her, "Don't worry, everything is fine. I donated a lung and a kidney and now you have to call me Dad." Of course we all laughed! I was released after a thorough examination, but laughter proved the best medicine as it did many times during our years as van partners.

We had a regular route so D.T.E.S. people would have a general time to expect us to arrive, although some days so many emergency interventions interrupted our schedule that we didn't make it. Seizures, overdoses on the street or in a hotel and acute traumas while we were on the spot (fights, traffic injuries or other life-threatening situations) were common. Priority action was uppermost and we would notify the W.I.S.H. Society, along with other regular stops, of any delay or inability to attend.

In some cases we would arrange a special visit off-schedule. The person who wanted to see us would walk to another stop on our map or I would be able to determine what action was necessary by phone. In some cases what I learned on the phone meant a quick call to Emergency Services for transfer to the hospital from the person's location. More often the need was minor and all I had to do was to suggest that the person attend Native Health or the Downtown Clinic, both of which are open in the early evening.

Bulk bags of Jolly Ranchers and red licorice twists were always in my backpack for "atta boys and girls," but they had other uses too. I once gave a Jolly Rancher to a diabetic who was "tweaking out" on crack. The rule of thumb when determining an insulin reaction or a diabetic reaction is, "When in doubt, give sugar."

Recovery from too much insulin (an insulin reaction) can be initiated quickly with a drink of juice or a candy. If the person continues to exhibit anxiety and aggressiveness and does not calm down within a few minutes after the sweet treat, the possibility is a diabetic reaction (too much sugar). Because a diabetic reaction carries with it a danger of slipping quickly into a coma this situation becomes an immediate emergency. The person may be on the street but requires insulin adjustment and is moved by E.H.S. to hospital.

Tweaking from cocaine or meth addiction looks quite similar to the agitation and aggressive symptoms of insulin reaction, and the sweetness provides some relief. Having the person sit and chat for fifteen or twenty minutes gave me time to observe their reaction to the candy. It is similar to having an allergy shot or donating blood—sit for a few minutes to rule out a reaction to the procedure. Tweakers will continue to thrash their arms and legs about but are likely to have moments of control and you may be able to get them to agree to go to detox or safe housing. But in the long run, candy is dandy if drugs ain't handy.

We occasionally saw the odd patient wheeling an IV pole downtown just to get a smoke. We stopped and returned the person to St. Paul's when we saw them, often because we were asked by the hospital to keep an eye out for them. Many patients in hospital told us they were dying for a smoke more than for a "fix." I carried a pack of cigarettes in my pocket and I left a few with the patient or we took them out to the roof garden smoking area. The instructions were always the same: take a couple of puffs, extinguish, keep the leftovers and make them last. Hey, if a cigarette would keep them there for treatment, it's part of the harm intervention process. They were getting treatment for personal medical issues, lessening the possible spread of infectious disease to others in the community. The benefit outweighed the hazard and we did not reward negative behaviour.

Our hospital visits were made in the late afternoon on Sundays and Wednesdays, before our W.I.S.H. stop at 6:30 PM daily. St. Paul's was the main stop but we did go to Vancouver General Hospital (V.G.H.) and G.F. Strong Physical Rehab when a visit was requested or we learned that one of "our people" had been admitted.

We initiated one memorable visit to Vancouver General Hospital Emergency when we received a call from a nurse there, who asked us to attend because a patient was refusing treatment unless "Bonnie is here." Jimmy was always a bit difficult to communicate with rationally and his paranoid ideation complicated matters further.

He was a regular visitor to the van and the Brandiz Hotel pub. Jimmy tugged a portable O_2 tank along with him everywhere he went to stabilize his Chronic Obstructive Pulmonary Disease (C.O.P.D.). This particular day he was having a beer in the pub and forgot to turn off his tank. He lit a cigarette and turned into a human torch with flames shooting out his nostrils through the nasal tubing. OMG! Picture it! Fire in the hole! Staff and patrons took action very quickly, turning off his tank and covering his face with cold, wet cloths.

We went to V.G.H. immediately. The humorous part was that a cranky old nurse from the street in her jeans and hiking boots was asked to attend so the old bugger would cooperate with hospital staff. The good part was that he didn't die.

Manny and I were greeted happily by the doctor, the nursing staff and Jimmy. I bit my tongue and didn't ask him what he was all so fired up about—under normal circumstances we usually shared wisecracks with him. He yelled, "You're here!" and cooperated fully with the necessary intubation of his nose, IV fluid hookup and pain management. The damage could have been worse but was confined mainly to his nasal membranes and mid-face region. He was subsequently transferred to the burn unit, where isolation infection protocol was established—gowns, mask and gloves required for anyone entering his room. It is commonly called Reverse Isolation because it protects the patient from exposure to outside bacteria. We tried to visit every day we were on shift.

Jimmy recovered quite nicely after several weeks. But our song for that first evening was probably "Light My Fire," I suppose, or a perky round of the old camping tune, "Fire's burning, fire's burning, draw nearer, draw nearer."

The Health Van and the Rig Van met at the same busy stop twice every night—close to the Brandiz Hotel on Hastings, near Main. We made rendezvous there because of the volume of people requiring health care and support: medication, intervention, wound management, dressing changes for needle abscesses or trauma referral. The presence of both vans at the site allowed both services to be provided in safety, first from 8 PM to 9 PM and later from 10:30 PM to 11:30 PM. The Rig Van always parked in front of the Health Van, which allowed the Rig Van driver good visibility of the activity at the Health Van, and conversely, the Health Van driver could see the activity around the Rig Van. The Health Van dealt only with nursing assessment, treatments or referrals at this stop. All people requesting user supplies or condoms were told to go to the Rig Van.

Of course, there was always the odd person who didn't want to wait in line at the Rig Van and knew that we carried exchange supplies—but exchanges at the Health Van were limited to requests when the Rig Van was not in the immediate area. There was also a long line of people waiting for the Health Van doors to open and reveal my smiling face.

Manny handled triage outside the open side doors and, like in any emergency department, assessed according to urgency or need. He often called into the Van that somebody only needed a Tylenol, vitamins or lozenges. These were readily accessible so Manny could hand them to the client after checking with me and noting the first name of the person. This allowed me time to continue with a new wound treatment, a change of dressing or other duties that we deemed to be nursing priorities.

I always felt safe on the van; for any client who hassled me there were ten others who had something to say about it! I always had Manny—except one evening when I had a drunk in the van for a dressing change and the door was shut. I could hear Manny prioritizing a long line outside the door. My inebriated client wanted to show his appreciation before leaving and backed me against the fridge. I turned my head to avoid a kiss and received a wet one in the ear. *Yuk!* I opened the door to let the guy out and called Manny, but he had a hard time trying not to laugh while I Q-tipped my ear out with peroxide!

The "I was here first" approach did not work in the triage line-up—the individual either followed the rules or did without. Frequent flyers were generally cooperative and often told us of somebody who should be seen now! It often turned out to be an overdose in a lane or doorway in the 100 block of East Hastings, or an epileptic seizure. Many times Manny locked down the van, grabbed the emergency bag and he and I were on the move.

The bag contained pretty well all the supplies necessary for first response: portable O_2, airways, masks, major bleed supplies, splinting and support equipment. I cannot count the number of times we intervened in a life-threatening situation and managed to get action within the "golden hour"—that period of time medical personnel consider vital to surviving a major medical crisis. In that period of time the patient must be assessed and intervention begun before transport to hospital. Cases of serious bleeding trauma, overdose, unknown internal injuries or other health problems could certainly result in death without prompt onsite response and management to sustain life in a compromised person in acute distress.

We ran to attend an unconscious man on Carrall Street one evening. The rig was still in his arm and the tie in place. I removed the rig and tie and positioned him for breathing assistance. Manny announced that there was a pulse but there was no evidence of respiration. Manny called 911 while I prepared to ensure oxygenation via airway, bag and mask. I measured how long the airway needed to be along the outside of the patient's lower jaw toward his ear. We didn't want him compromised further by using the wrong size airway.

I called Manny for a green airway based on my measurement. He told me we were out of the green ones so he passed me the next size up. I inserted it carefully and tested it with the bag and mask. I noted air entry with the rising of the patient's chest so I continued assisted breathing until the paramedics arrived— after the fire department and police. It was an E.H.S. crew we did not recognize as originating from the D.T.E.S.

The paramedic asked me, "Who inserted the airway?"

I replied, "I did."

To which he responded, "You used the wrong size!"

I said, "Yes, I know, and it is inserted with that in mind, you'll notice."

At that point a fireman interjected, "Listen, we use what we have on the street and make it work, so don't hassle our nurse."

It was always a team approach with the D.T.E.S. services. Some lives were saved and some were not.

Actually dealing with a life emergency on the street was, in retrospect, automatic for me and also for Manny. It was scary sometimes just thinking about what we had been through. We had to talk—sometimes before we barfed, sometimes after. While verbally debriefing after handing patients over to E.H.S. we determined we had similar feelings toward our actions, required applications, focus, control and the result of our interventions.

We saw upward of seventy-five clients every night. Our numbers rose before welfare cheque day, often to more than 100 clients, most of whom were suffering from withdrawal discomfort. Requests were for Tylenol, ibuprofen, vitamins, Maalox—and from my personal stash, Jolly Rancher candies or red liquorice!

Trust reigned supreme in the D.T.E.S. I was "Mommy" to my clients—naughtiness was firmly addressed verbally and hugs were given when warranted. Manny and I always clarified the consequences of client behaviour or motivation in an eye-level, up-front manner. No secret maps or false promises: the glass is half-full, not half-empty. It was the decision of the client as to whether the consequence would be good or bad and would ultimately affect the person alone. It might result in a disappointing outcome or an exciting small step forward but we never disregarded either—we did not enable, but encouraged with truth and trust.

Hey, it didn't always work out the way we wanted every time, but we knew and the people knew that our backs were never turned on them. Regardless of the choices and their good or bad consequences, the seed was planted and fertilized as indicated. It was left to the addicted to make the decision: seek recovery or continue in their entrenched existence.

I have to mention that there were many memorial services at Glenhaven Memorial Chapel on East Hastings. Often the only people attending were Liz James the street nurse, me and the clergy who carried out the full service for us. On most occasions it was an open casket service, allowing us to pay our respects and shed a tear or two. Janine from M.P.A. Court Services joined us one day and we were really happy to see that someone had taken special time to corn-row a beloved client's long black hair—a sign of true cultural respect.

Eighteen:
No Place Like Home

The reality behind homeless people in the downtown core is not limited to human beings caught up in the throes of addiction. The population of homeless is just that: homeless. Elderly or disabled people have also slipped through the cracks in the various government ministries and live their lives wrapped in blankets in a doorway, or live in the bug-infested filth of a Skid Row room. They are also homeless. A home is comfort, security, companionship and a supportive environment where those who are incapacitated by financial, physical and mental health issues have their basic human needs met instead of going unnoticed day after day.

The top step of St. James on the corner of Cordova and Gore and the First United Church on the corner of Hastings and Gore are safe places for our marginalized citizens. The compassionate heartbeats of both places are intervention and advocacy for those who cannot speak for themselves.

We observed the lack of or abhorrent living conditions every night on the D.E.Y.A.S. Health Outreach Van. We initiated intervention wherever possible: made referrals on behalf of many people in an attempt to facilitate a connection, intervention and possibly an advocacy resolution through agencies appropriate to the individual needs of the downtown core.

Let's be realistic, as I mentioned earlier. Aside from hospital transportation to address threatening health issues, the only services available at midnight were the nurse and driver on the D.E.Y.A.S. Health Outreach Van. We provided socks; blankets; dry, warm clothing from "Bonnie's Boutique" in the rear of the van and somebody to listen and commiserate. I would be lying if I said we were always greeted with open arms. Perseverance and stops "just to say hello" were required to gain people's trust so they would accept us and let us assist in some way.

D.E.Y.A.S. advocated interventions based on our experiences in the Health Outreach Van, directing them to a specific agency or service. John Turvey, the founder and executive director of D.E.Y.A.S. until his retirement, followed these up diligently. He was like a dog with a bone with the Downtown Eastside Residents' Association (D.E.R.A.) when informed about disease-ridden rooms visited or seen by the Health Outreach Van or by D.E.Y.A.S. counsellors.

One request that stands out in my mind was from the Downtown Health Clinic's physician, asking us to check on a client of his after the clinic's hours of operation. A particular elderly woman, whom I will refer to as Martha, had not shown up at the D.H.C. for a necessary follow-up to her health problems, so I was asked to make an assessment visit to her room at a D.E.R.A. designated housing facility.

Manny and I entered the building reception area with its clean, highly polished floors and a notice board adorned with a photograph of an elected Vancouver city council member. The duty desk clerk told me that Martha would have to come down to the lobby to see me. I clarified the reason for my visit, the fact that the patient was known to be barely able to walk and the need for privacy for the health assessment, but the clerk informed me that no visitors were permitted beyond the foyer. I said that we were there at the request of Martha's physician at the Downtown Clinic, that we would be attending to her needs in her room based on a professional referral, that we would undertake the necessary health treatments or hospital transfer if we deemed it necessary and that if they liked we would call the V.P.D. to confirm our need to attend, and marched to the elevator. Amazingly we were suddenly allowed to go.

Manny and I entered the elevator and proceeded to the third floor of the residence. It did not take long to locate Martha's room. The putrid, rancid smell served as a G.P.S. locator as soon as the elevator door opened.

Martha was living in absolute filth, with cockroaches and vermin in abundance. The smell of excrement, rotting food and other garbage was so offensive that Manny began gagging. He left the room to sit in the stairwell until I was finished. Martha was dirty, with open sores in a septic state, possibly from insect bites combined with very poor personal hygiene. Her general health and mental status required transfer to hospital.

I informed John Turvey the following day of the issue and he initiated communication with the residential facility and

D.E.R.A. without delay. Martha was not an addicted person or a working girl on the street. She was an elderly woman with limited mental capacity due to aging, unable to care or speak for herself. I perceived her as homeless just by the conditions of her housing.

For many compromised people, a place to sleep safely with reasonable access and relative comfort was under the Georgia Viaduct or Burrard Street Bridge rather than in many kinds of Skid Row housing. For others, the deep woods of Stanley Park gave a sense of peace and Mother Nature comforting. I have visited a few such dwellings over the years. The clean cardboard flooring and blanket walls, in my opinion, earned a two-star rating compared to some of the deplorable rooms offered and supported by our tax dollars. Under a bridge or in Stanley Park may also be the only home these people know, the only spot they can find to satisfy a basic human need—Home.

Nineteen:
Sex, Drugs and
Rock 'n' Roll

D.E.Y.A.S. was a small storefront with a garish red-painted metal grill covering the window and featuring a park bench out front. The door and trim were the same bright red. No flashing arrow saying, "Junkies enter here" visible, just the simple words painted on the front window: Downtown Eastside Youth Activities Society.

Visiting the original D.E.Y.A.S. storefront on Main St. in 2009

Once inside there were two doors: one leading into the D.E.Y.A.S. office, and one up a steep staircase that led to the street nurses' office for onsite consulting, examination, treatment and education about transmission and harm reduction relating to sexually transmitted diseases (S.T.Ds) and HIV. They were funded by City of Vancouver Health and Provincial Health Services.

Liz, the nurse mentioned earlier (in my holding cell years), worked out of that onsite facility. D.E.Y.A.S. and the S.T.D. street nurses enjoyed a very good working relationship. The street nurses often came down to use our copying equipment and I went upstairs to attend monthly "brown bag" lunch meetings—always held on a welfare day because people had money and we usually weren't as busy.

These meetings were attended by many services in the D.T.E.S., not just the nurses. It was often a pretty well packed selection of various D.T.E.S. services. Greater Vancouver Mental Health, Native Health Care workers, Carnegie Centre, Powell Place for Women and Children, May's Place (palliative care), the W.I.S.H. Centre, Vancouver Coastal Health and V.A.N.D.U. (Vancouver Association of Drug Users) came together to share different experiences on the street relating to drug abuse and potentially harmful substances, and to brainstorm methods of harm reduction and curbing endemic infectious diseases and S.T.Ds. Lots of "Have you seen... lately?"

We teamed cooperatively in situations where all service representatives expressed worries. One in particular involved street women who had not been seen over a very long period of time. The D.E.Y.A.S. Rig Van, the Health Van, W.I.S.H., V.A.N.D.U., Native Health Services and the Vancouver street nurses certainly covered hours and areas where and when these women were normally seen. Our fears for these missing women intensified as the list grew to more than sixty-five names. A few were located safe out of province or in prison facilities or hospitals, but as for the rest...

Many of the women working under pimps sometimes went on a "tour circuit" provincially while others who might have been under the control of gangs travelled from Vancouver down the west coast to Seattle, San Francisco, Los Angeles and Hawaii. Some of these prostitutes were used as mules to move drugs for their "bosses."

The Health Van developed a system that had some success. We asked the working girls to leave a message on our Van phone or with the Rig Van driver if they were going to be away for a certain length of time. It worked quite well with "high track" non-addicted hookers but not as well with the addicted.

The Health Van not only visited call girls and escorts on the high track (in the hotel district and around Renfrew Street), but also made three regular trips through the stroll every night. We would slow the Van for corners with one or more girls, offer a "bad date sheet" and ask if they needed anything, like bandaids, Tylenol or condoms. If we didn't see a girl in her usual spot, maybe she was "on a date," but when we didn't see them for several runs and days we expected the worst.

Geographically, the stroll stretched from Gore and Cordova to Renfrew Street. The areas were quite easily designated: there were addict areas, a "tranny" (transvestite) area and the kiddy stroll (girls as young as twelve). The younger girls were often watched by a pimp. The streets we covered were primarily in the warehouse areas along the waterfront. There was no "as the crow flies" to our route—we wove in and out and up and down each trip.

On one particular trip, we saw a tranny under the Heatley overpass who was being yelled at and harassed by a group of about six youths between nine and fourteen years old. We saw them walking by and yelling at her as we rounded the corner. She spoke very little English, was by herself and visibly frightened. I got out of the Van to talk to her and a little guy in the group hollered excitedly, "Hey, there's the Van; they give out condoms!"

I immediately yelled back, "Yes, you're right, sonny, but first you need to have a penis!" The group started to laugh and point yuk-yuks at the boy and carried on their way.

Once on a late run Manny and I noticed a girl standing on a corner under a tree in a poorly-lit area. Neither of us recognized her; she looked very young. I rolled down the window and gave her my standard phrase, "Hi, everything okay? Do you need anything?" "Anything" meant condoms, bandaids, etc. The girl just shook her head no.

I said, "We have a new bad date sheet for you to read over," and held it out the window. She came over to the window and I whispered to her quickly that we had not seen her before. "How old are you? Is someone watching you?"

She replied, "I'm twelve... first time... I gotta go." She was visibly nervous as I gave her the sheet and a business card with our phone number.

I said to her as she walked away, "We are through here regularly. Call if you need anything."

She turned and said quietly, "Pray for me." We noticed an Asian fellow leaning against a tree kitty-corner to where we had been as we drove away. My eyes filled with tears.

Manny got on the phone to the D.E.Y.A.S. Youth Car and passed the information on to the worker there. The Youth Car made every effort to follow up on youth, offering safe housing, rides home and supportive measures young people may not have been aware existed. Most important, the youngster had someone to trust who would care for and help them whenever needed. Even if the youth refused any assistance, the Health Van and Youth Car continued to drive by each night to say hi. We never forgot to open the window of opportunity so that the child might hop into our vehicle.

Further along the stroll, in the high track, we talked to women who were working just to put food on the table or put themselves through university. These sex workers were more of the call girl than the streetwalker type, with no addiction issues. Some carried cell phones for "good phone" services by Visa or Mastercard! They enjoyed visiting us for supplies and harm reduction information. One particular girl came to work for a short time on the Health Van as a relief nurse after she graduated from nursing school.

Many people see prostitution as a source of income for females only. A stop with the van in a four-block stretch starting at 700 Seymour would make citizens aware of "Boys' Town"—a substantial population of young men working the streets as a livelihood. We gave out many condoms and never forgot about the lads. Some of these young men were working the street to save for tuition to further their university education.

When handing out condoms we often tried to make the process memorable. We didn't always refer to condoms by nicknames but some well-known working girls and guys got a kick out of the ones we came out with. We tried, "Here's a nose cone for the rocket," "a bigger place to park your truck," "something to put on the big whopper" and "Incredible Bulk," to name a few. We used humour to educate because the dorky names were more likely to be remembered and passed on to others for a giggle. It was better to suggest harm reduction in a way they might remember than to have them pass on "the gift that keeps on giving," an S.T.D., which was no laughing matter. It went a step toward establishing an attitude of trust by reassuring them that they could talk to us about anything or anyone at any time.

In the early '80s a street nurse named Liz visited our holding cells occasionally to touch base with me and follow up on recently arrested prisoners. She was mandated under the Department of Venereal Disease Control to medicate any person in custody named as a possible on tracking lists given to her by working girls. The person was given a total of about six pills to take, privately, in her presence. An ounce of prevention is worth a pound of cure.

I saw Liz several times over the years after I took on the Health Van role: at meetings with service agencies, at memorial services for clients, and the odd time checking out the bars! She was so well respected, trusted and appreciated in her role. I recall a time when she handed out small boxes labelled "King Kong Kondom." We laughed about the name and the gorilla on the box but not about the need. I put one in my son's Christmas stocking that year. he didn't laugh, just gave me a startled fifteen-year-old look and a " Muuum!"

The working women were hard and fast on anyone found abusing or dealing drugs at the W.I.S.H. drop-in. It was their place and their rules were adhered to without exception in most cases—rules such as "No males without the knowledge and consent of the women," "No smoking inside," and

"Working girls only are permitted to participate in special activities or partake in daily hot suppers provided by staff and volunteers."

The working women protected W.I.S.H. They were quick to intervene in any situation that threatened the security and continuing operation of their drop-in, such as taking food out to "boyfriends," bringing in drug paraphernalia or abusing one of their peers or a volunteer. Sometimes they demanded a woman leave the building because she broke the rules. The women even requested that certain women be banned permanently from W.I.S.H. I must say there were several cases over the years when actual physical confrontations took place over the rules. Staff or volunteers were usually able to resolve the problem by asking the offender to leave or comply. But once in a while even I was called in to break up an altercation.

Addicts sometimes referred to rigs (syringes and needles) as "points." One of the key functions of both D.E.Y.A.S. vans was to exchange new rigs for used ones. Such exchanges were an important method of harm reduction and prevention of the transmission of hepatitis and HIV. It was the primary service in the job description of a Rig Van driver.

Addicts were never refused a new rig but the D.E.Y.A.S. employees at the exchange walk-in on Main Street, the Rig Van drivers and the Health Van driver always asked where their used ones were. We heard, "Oh, I didn't plan on using today," "I left it at home," "My girlfriend has them and she's working," "I just got out of jail," and many more excuses. The drivers gave clients new rigs and reminded them to turn the used ones in to the office, Rig Van or Health Van.

The Rig Van was on the street on a twenty-four-hour shift rotation. The driver was always an employee of D.E.Y.A.S., an addict in recovery for a minimum of two years. The drivers were a valuable connection for on-the-spot communication with the Health Van and the D.E.Y.A.S. Youth Car.

The supplies on the Rig Van consisted of small containers of sterile water, cleansing wipes, cotton swabs, small containers of Hibitane antibacterial cleanser and handouts that alerted users about dangerous drug combinations such as cocaine mixed with heroin or contamination of street drugs with Javex, rat poison or numerous other "cuts" (substances added by the dealers before the drugs hit the street pusher).

Rig Van drivers covered a long, regular route: along the waterfront to the outskirts of Stanley Park, as far east as Boundary Road, south to Kingsway and west to Burrard Street. They responded to direct calls to collect used drug abuse paraphernalia from beaches, schoolyards or parks, along with calls for supplies or collection from other services like doctors and clinics. These were arranged by phone, as were visits to exchange used rigs for new for addicted professionals in the upper echelons of society.

D.E.Y.A.S. was discreet and confidential in every facet of its duties. The name of any person was never mentioned. It was a policy firmly adhered to by D.E.Y.A.S. as a matter of professional ethics.

Clients were warned that they should always know who they were buying from. The response, "Oh, I'm not using, I'm just smoking weed," just didn't work. By the time I left the Health Van, marijuana was being spiked with meth or crack by some dealers, and the "weed only" user woke up wired soon enough.

Addicts were often warned about strong potency or deadly additives to street drugs. Heroin was a prime example: street drugs often featured toxic additives thought to enhance the desired effect. A cap was seldom more than ten percent pure heroin. The remaining additives, or "cut," could be milk sugar, or toxins such as arsenic or strychnine. Colour changes to the injectable powder could indicate that ephedrine, Gravol or rat poison had been added. Horse tranquilizer—a generic ketamine preparation—was also used as a cut. It surprised more than a few addicts with a permanent exit from our world.

Arsenic is not excreted by the body. It just keeps accumulating until the toxic level is sufficient to kill you. Strychnine is partially excreted but it can trigger renal failure, resulting in death. Heroin addicts are aware of the cut but the poison enhances the high and that's what they wanted.

The gift or sale of a "hot cap" to a user was also done to take care of business, so to speak. If an addict was deemed a rat or was thought to have been ripping off a dealer in some way, a street order would come down to provide a pure substance for the addict's personal hit. This ensured the business was taken care of permanently.

Sadly, hard core addicts often told me that they were not concerned about dying. A lot of them said, "I know. But if I die orgasmic, on the end of a needle, that's the way to go."

One of the important aspects of intravenous addiction in most long-term users, male and female, was and is still the ritual around the addiction. The rituals take several forms. The "cops and robbers" feeling while purchasing the illicit substance triggers the high. The ritual of cooking the drug and tying off the vein increases the anticipation of the fix. These rituals can remain as triggers after detoxification and will not be resolved or controlled unless there is an effective recovery support program executed immediately following the acute physical detoxification. That way the addict learns acceptable ways of coping with his or her specific triggers.

It doesn't work if addicts enter a detox facility to manage the physical symptoms of withdrawal and are denied the opportunity or are unwilling to address the reasons behind their addictions. Too many voluntary detox admissions are determined effective by the addicted person merely to reduce a high cost habit to a temporarily lower level and get off more cheaply. Perhaps it is part of personal financial recession intervention?

A similar way of reducing their addiction and "starting all over" at a cheaper cost was opting for incarceration on an outstanding charge. The decision is win–win for addicts: they have dealt with the charges, served time and detoxed under medical intervention. They are released and can anticipate the first high again at a lower cost, a depressing fact that occurs over and over if facilities, support and motivation to make a change are not present.

I have seen it many times over the years, where users enter an acute detox facility in the downtown core, stay for approximately seven days and then are released out the front door into the centre of the addiction community.

If there is nobody to scoop them up and take them out of the area for support and counselling over a longer period of time, "detoxed" people may as well be standing naked in their addiction saying, "Pick me, pick me..." to the dealers. Detox by itself is merely a hiatus; the reasons for addiction are right in their faces again. They are destined to relapse in over ninety-nine percent of cases without continued treatment in a reputable recovery facility away from the addiction core.

Professionals, often addicts in recovery for a long period of time, address the ritual "triggers" as part of the recovery process.

A simple phone call to the Health Van, D.E.Y.A.S. counsellors or a recovery house might have been all that is required for a motivated client. A call from the detox facility and the "physically" withdrawn person met at the door and transported to a program away from the "triggers" in the Downtown Eastside. If it creates a positive result in one percent of addicts in the program it is a successful intervention.

From 2000 to 2003 the use of drugs and alcohol in combination reached proportions beyond epidemic. Illicit drug use combined with alcohol became endemic. Obviously this was most visible in Skid Row areas but invisibly existed at all levels of our society.

Not only that, but drug users have become younger and younger. It is no longer the teenaged lemon gin experimentation of the Sixties. The mean age of youth entrenched in addiction is now twelve years with little variance between genders, among cultures or societal levels. Children addicted at birth represent the extreme in this trend.

Infants who are born addicted to opiates or barbiturates require a lot of one-on-one attention. Rocking, protective warmth and cuddling are very important for easing the physical withdrawal discomfort the baby experiences following birth. The tiny human being is as addicted to drugs as his birth mother, although certainly not of his own choosing. The complex process of detoxification and organ function development eclipses the normal birth trauma any newborn may experience. Some infants have to be transferred to Sunny Hill Children's Hospital for extended special care.

In many critical care nurseries, there are volunteers (with a capital V!) who attend to the babies on a regular schedule. They come in to hold the swaddled infants and rock them. The program has proven to be effective in easing the pain of withdrawal. What child does not require cuddling, rocking and the comfort of warm arms when they are hurting?

Many of the volunteers are in the grandma and grandpa age bracket. There are some wonderful "Grandmas" and "Grandpas" involved in meeting this very basic human need. The nursing staff in the unit is stretched to the limit with intervention and regular duties.

Volunteers give of themselves in so many areas of great need and sorrow. Their strength and dedication speaks volumes for those who are employed in areas of stress and anxiety. God bless volunteers… How could we manage without these oft-unsung heroes? The emotional rewards, shared by all, are therapeutic and everlasting.

In some cases, it was a blessing for a mother to be incarcerated for an offence. The result was appropriate monitoring of the pregnancy along with hospital registration in preparation for a possible high-risk birth.

The mother-to-be's fear and anxiety associated with birthing an addicted baby could be dealt with by choosing one of two options: denial and non-compliance with prenatal care, or a willingness to accept medical monitoring of the pregnancy out of concern for the unborn.

A fetus is deemed, by law, to be a non-viable living being until the third trimester. The innocent child is a victim at birth regardless of which path the mother takes. It is only a matter of degree of victimization. Which path will be taken by the mom-to-be? Medical abortions are primarily limited to the first and second trimesters—up to the twenty-sixth week—and should not be used as a form of birth control.

A pregnant addict on the street may make her choices based on the advice of professionals she knows and trusts. Often the professional is a street nurse or a physician in a clinic in the downtown core. However, it is a decision that the mom-to-be makes. The medical staff simply monitors following their assessment of the patient's determination and compliancy, and registers the mother-to-be for the birth (usually at B.C. Women's and Children's Hospital because it will be high risk).

The major concern for care providers was, and probably is still, the pregnant addicted women we don't know are out there shooting up, along with the women who are resistant to any kind of intervention. Serious survival and birthing challenges are faced by unknowing medical staff in such situations.

Methadone maintenance programs, prescribed under strict supervision through designated clinics, have been considered a safe treatment decision for the compliant, responsible addict in the past. Methadone is sometimes given to pregnant women under strict supervision by a physician specializing in methadone treatment.

Both the medical staff and the patient must be strongly committed to the treatment program to be effective. It is an alternative to total drug withdrawal that can take place outside of a treatment facility, but it is not without potential hazards.

Methadone is a pure narcotic with a maintenance level that can be gradually attained so the discomfort of withdrawal can be alleviated. Any abuse of illicit drugs along with the prescribed methadone could compromise the health and likely survival of anyone on the program.

Methadone users still require supportive counselling because on methadone maintenance there are none of the buzzed, orgasmic feelings that the addict previously enjoyed. There is instead a feeling of wellness without the high. Dealing with the addict's craving for the high must be part of the monitoring.

The positive side of methadone is that although the person is on a pure substance program, a gradually achieved maintenance dose will ease the basic cellular pain of withdrawal and allow the addict to manage his or her addiction. Many people on methadone are on small doses and can be employed successfully.

Street narcotics have no maintenance level. The craving persists. The more you use, the more you want. The habit increases along with the danger of poisoning by the contaminants in the street drug.

We cannot ignore the fact that the eventual withdrawal from methadone is a challenge to be addressed by care providers and patients alike. The watchword for care providers is to expect the unexpected. Unsupervised withdrawal from methadone, just like from heroin, can be life-threatening. Gradual lowering of the dosage with medical supervision and control is a viable plan for a determined addict who wants to be drug-free. Withdrawal is managed in much the same way as achieving the maintenance level but is achieved in reverse order—lowering the dose gradually.

It is a slow go in some cases because methadone is pure and there are health issues that must be heeded. It is important to be aware of any "piggyback" use of illicit narcotics while coming off methadone.

Twenty:
Teaching the Seamy Side
of Nursing

I counted it as a good step forward when the Health Van service was asked to provide some community education to senior student nurses from various training schools—Langara College, Kwantlen College, Camosun College, the University of B.C. and Douglas College. Pre-medical students also rode along from time to time but the bulk of our ridealongs were student nurses from Douglas College. By the term bulk, I don't mean that we saw how many nurses we could cram into the Health Van on a given day! It was one student on each scheduled day.

The initial request for the Van to be part of the education program came from Fran, a senior instructor from Douglas College who had learned of the D.E.Y.A.S. van and had accompanied Manny and me on a shift. She was amazed at the volume of D.T.E.S. people who attended for various routine requests—Tylenol, lozenges, hand wipes, a hi–bye chat, and the provision of safe sex products along with "rig exchanges" (new needles for used ones). We were more than willing when we were asked to permit ridealong students as part of the students' community experience.

Nursing student orientation began at 2:30 PM at the D.E.Y.A.S. office. Ridealong nights were a real eye-opener to nursing students. I always made a point of introducing the students to the clients. In most cases, this dispelled any adverse ideation. I do not recall any street person ever being rude to a student. In most cases they said, "Hi! Do you think you might want to work down here?"

By the 8 PM Brandiz Hotel stop, the students' eyes were not popping out of their heads and their nervousness had pretty well abated; after all, by that point they had already been conditioned and reassured for four hours! The students did not treat clients—they observed and asked me (and in some cases a willing patient) questions during a treatment procedure. They always wore surgical gloves and no name tags while observing or when we were making a home visit. The reasons are self-explanatory: harm reduction for the student and general personal safety. They did not wear gloves on hospital visits—they were well trained in sanitation and hand care stations were readily available there.

Ridealongs provided an experience that could never be learned in a classroom or in a downtown clinic setting. The students saw the D.T.E.S. through different eyes; during hardships, desperation and deprivation in the dark, nasty hours. They met a segment of society as human beings, with human feelings and human pain. The students' nervousness was replaced with compassion, empathy and dismay. Most important, they left with the knowledge that addiction is an illness, and that mental health in the D.T.E.S. is indeed a health problem.

My hope was that the experience would also enlighten the students that "a broken leg is still a broken leg." When a patient arrives in the emergency department for treatment, ask the question about drug use, of course, but treat the broken leg as you would any other patient's broken leg!

I saw some young nurses who were burnt out in their working area, especially in St. Paul's Hospital, where most of our clients were sent. There was the odd time when Manny and I transported a client with a medical problem that required a physician's assessment.

One particular incident stands out in my mind. A man had been in an altercation with another outside Carnegie Centre on the corner of Main and Hastings. The Van was parked near the Brandiz Hotel at the time and a friend brought "Gil" to us. He had sustained a severe laceration to the face and concussive trauma to the head when he fell to the pavement. We learned from witnesses that he did not lose consciousness, got up by himself and showed no problem with speech or orientation. A cleansing and pressure dressing was applied, blood pressure and pulse taken. His pupil response appeared equal and reactive to light.

Carnegie Centre

I filled out referral information and asked Manny to call a taxi to take him to Emergency for suturing and assessment. Gil's immediate response was, "I'm not going to any fucking hospital. They won't do anything and they treat me like shit!"

Manny and I asked him if he would go to the hospital if we went with him. We didn't make it a practice of actually taking clients ourselves in the Van. We normally called E.H.S. or gave out a to-and-from taxi transfer, paid for by D.E.Y.A.S. In this case the man needed treatment and he agreed, so away we went to St. Paul's Emergency. I must mention here that St. Paul's Hospital is located in the downtown core of Vancouver and is a very busy hospital. It goes without saying that many of the patients they see are from the Skid Row area of Vancouver. I have empathy for them because they are overworked and understaffed. The influx of people under the influence of a substance (be it alcohol or drugs) can be overwhelming and puts a great strain on nurses especially.

A security officer approached as we entered behind Gil and told him to leave: "You were here last week." The officer was not aware that we were with Gil so we identified ourselves and clarified our reason for being there with him. A young nurse called his name and we stood outside the curtain while she completed the nursing intake. We heard the nurse speak to him in a very condescending fashion, telling him, "You will be treated without any pain medication because you are an addict." The man hadn't even asked for any at this point!

I asked to speak to the young nurse privately afterward, and asked, "Why did you speak to him in that way?"

Her response was, "We get them in here all the time, manipulating the system for drugs."

I shared with her that I had over thirty years of nursing in my chosen area and I wasn't as burnt out as she was. I continued, "I find it sad that after such a short time working in your chosen field, you display a lack of respect and professionalism while caring for a trauma patient." I gave her my card and asked her to call me and go for a ridealong with us. She did not.

We really enjoyed our visits to the infectious/communicable diseases and palliative care wards on the tenth floor of St. Paul's Hospital. The nurses on the tenth floor were incredible and I'm sure still are! These nurses were there because that's where they want to be. They understood their patients and always treated them with respect and dignity. The work site was busy, with strong emotions and open feelings shared among patients and staff.

I am not saying that the addicts being treated there were given everything they asked for. They were given everything they needed as ordered by the physician. The nursing was genuine, honest and professional. The patients trusted and accepted the care with appreciation. Several of the long-time nurses would ask me about former patients and how they were doing following their discharge.

I tried to schedule student nurse ridealongs for Wednesdays to meet patients on the two units we visited regularly. I loved taking nursing students to the tenth floor! I made a point of telling the student that Manny was D.E.F.C., so be sure to listen to his important instructions when the elevator door opened. The student usually waited a while after we entered the elevator before asking what D.E.F.C. meant. It certainly helped them relax when I said, "Designated Elevator Fart Checker," and they burst out laughing.

Another Douglas College nursing instructor, Brenda, learned about the "wonderful" experience students were having on the Health Van. Brenda rode with Manny and me and subsequently filled spaces that Fran hadn't booked, allowing her students to participate. It became a very popular request by students. Both instructors were astounded by the written assignments submitted about their students' experiences. Manny and I enjoyed the letters of appreciation. The popularity of the nursing student rides increased with requests from other nursing programs such as the University of B.C's degree program, Kwantlen College, Camosun College and Langara College.

One nurse did the ride and then requested through the college that she be permitted to do her preceptureship for her

Masters' degree in nursing on the Health Van. I had to provide documentation prior to approval that involved identifying liability, theory and concepts along with in-depth details of my own personal experience and credibility.

When the student commenced her program with us she developed several ideas to put into use on the van. Her insight into possible ways to improve and follow up referrals and communication was excellent. We gladly put her ideas into protocol on completion of her tenure.

One of the items she developed was a referral pad in a colour-coded three-part format. The white original went to the service the client was referred to, while the client being referred kept the yellow and the Health Van filed the pink. Simple check boxes for agencies we most often referred clients to were printed on the slips: Downtown Health Clinic, Centre for Disease Control, Vancouver Detox, Hospital, Mental Health Units, Vancouver Housing and "other." The forms were letterheaded as D.E.Y.A.S. Health Outreach and included a small area for referral reason. It was very helpful for communicating with specific services and allowed them to contact the Health Van for further information, clarification and follow-up.

I often received calls from emergency physicians regarding follow-up treatment of clients, such as wound intervention orders or dressings. If daily intravenous medication was necessary, I phoned the hospital to arrange a time for the client to attend. We then organized getting the client to the hospital for the procedure and we were called when the procedure was done. No admission or overnight hospital stay needed, and eased the nurses' workload. When the IV treatment was complete the hospital usually called or left us instructions outlining what ongoing wound management the Health Van needed to provide on the street. It didn't work for all clients but many were in enough pain to be compliant. The referral forms definitely improved communication with the emergency departments and other services.

Twenty-one:
Insite, Onsite or No Site?

There has been great controversy regarding the need, geographical location and lack of progressive intervention towards changing the addiction picture in the Downtown Eastside. One of the initiatives I believe can go a long way toward making that picture brighter is Insite, a storefront safe injection facility near Main and Hastings staffed by professional nurses, counsellors and other support workers. Insite has been in place since 2003. Onsite, a related facility, is located upstairs in the same building. Its twelve beds provide a starting point for addicts who wish to begin detox and managed withdrawal.

The Insite safe injection site actually opened prior to 2003, supervised by a volunteer nurse. It shut down for an assessment period and re-opened in 2003 with a formidably documented mission and less-than-formidable funding.

All levels of government need Insite. It is necessary as a permanent service. Six-month-at-a-time funding is absolute nonsense, Prime Minister Stephen Harper. I cheer the B.C. Supreme Court ruling that says the program allows addicts "to inject their illegal drugs in a safe, medically-supervised environment (which) is a matter of sensible healthcare… " Insite's future may end up in the Supreme Court of Canada for resolution but until then it will continue service.

I was the full-time nurse on the D.E.Y.A.S. Health Van. I and my driver, an addict in recovery for over ten years, worked out of the Downtown Eastside for many years—the nasty hours from 2:00 PM until 1:30 AM. Only one elected official ever rode along with me on a shift. A high-ranking member of the former Greater Vancouver Regional Health Board once said to me, "Bonnie, you are on the Health Outreach Van; we must have a chat sometime." My response was, "No, Dr. —, you must ride along with me sometime." He never did either, chat or ride. (Interestingly, the only politician who took me up on such an offer was Monique Begin, during her tenure as federal minister of native affairs. She was with us for several hours and even sat down for dinner with the gals at W.I.S.H. A neat lady!)

Forget about the "Four Pillars Approach" (prevention, treatment, harm reduction and enforcement) that the City of Vancouver uses, for now. The approach is currently more like an upside-down pyramid with no foundation. Instead, dump it in the circular file. Use a wagon wheel symbol with Insite as the focal point, branching out with services in a circle in all directions. Insite would be the hub, expanding to a circle connecting harm reduction, referral access, intervention, detox, treatment and recovery—the latter three geographically removed from the D.T.E.S. Full circle communication and action.

There has already been too much time (more than five years) and money (who knows how much) wasted on the so-called Four Pillars. Ask the people who work on the Downtown Eastside streets instead of wasting tax dollars on a whim. Get the truth from those who know the truth, and educate the ones who hold the purse strings.

The dedication and experience of the physicians and ground level nurses at Insite and Onsite are evident. Proof is there that the facilities save lives and the opportunity to expand and combine services by improving communication has always been there. Ask, listen and do instead of scattering money. The various levels of government have holes in their money buckets and we're way overdue for a new bucket. Patching the bucket we have is delaying further action and killing people who could be rescued.

The Insite/Onsite location just west of Main and Hastings is perfect for initial contact, counselling and education. The Insite hours are good and the staff is excellent and knowledgeable. D.E.R.A., the Centre for Disease Control and other

Getting a hug from a former Health Van client in front of Insite, 2009

dedicated services are nearby to provide information and networking contacts, and they work well together. But a comprehensive step-by-step process with compliance and consequence must exist for the system to truly help addicts.

Make the addict accountable for meeting specific goals, and if he or she does not, then have appropriate consequences in place. Insite is a service that should be the foundation of the Pillars, not the entire structure. Build on it—don't just use it as just a safe place to inject an unknown, illegal street substance. By "building" I am saying that there must be intervention, detox, treatment and recovery attached to Insite's first step. Onsite's follow-up is a major next step in ensuring a positive outcome for addicts.

At its maximum, addiction ultimately gives no buzz or high. The drug becomes just a way to keep from getting sick. The addict has maxed out. Now every cell and hair follicle is in excruciating pain, so the addict requires the drug just to function. The addict's desperation at this point provides an opening, which can lead to detox, treatment and recovery, and not to further personal destruction and endangerment to society.

Many addicts have reached this fork in the road. But until they can see a clear path—facilities in place, accessible and structured toward recovery without drug abuse—both forks in the road lead to disaster and so does the government's "harm reduction" measure. Harm reduction is just a political phrase meant to blind the taxpayer.

Releasing addicts directly onto the very same street from Detox, as is done now, merely scratches the surface of addiction. Addicts might as well be standing naked out there, within walking distance of the people with the illicit drugs that provided a cover for the deep-seated reasons behind addiction in the first place. Collect these extremely fragile people at the Detox door upon their release, take them directly to treatment away from the Downtown Eastside and move them progressively toward a recovery program. All three programs—detox, transition and recovery—require supervision in a controlled, progressive living environment.

The issues behind a person's drug use and addiction are still present following Detox, and the drugs and a place to fix are just around the corner. Detox is merely a scab over the wound of addiction. Relapse is inevitable without aggressive action by experienced people who can provide support and alternate coping skills, thus helping the addict to find a positive route to recovery.

Admittedly, safe injection sites can be seen as a method of harm reduction but it is a fart in a windstorm if it isn't part of a holistic approach: treating the whole person. The holistic approach has been an integral part of disease treatment for centuries. This approach is taught in every area of medical training. How is the holistic approach utilized in treating the disease of addiction? I can tell you it is not. The whole person is left out of intervention, assessment, treatment and recovery. Don't allow the public to see Insite as an enabling facility for drug abusers. Educate them!

The triggers creating the addiction need to be addressed—they have been present for many years. Recovery programs identify these triggers, and the addict in recovery is given more acceptable ways to deal with them to avoid relapse. It doesn't happen during the ten days of detox—if addicts stay that long—and it doesn't happen in Corrections, that's for sure. The triggers are not obvious and might be difficult to understand by the layperson. It might be the "cops and robbers" game, the rush to score the drug, the anticipation of the biggest high or the longest run on crystal meth, for example. Certain odours or even the nurse pumping up a blood pressure cuff—these might all trigger memories of drug use and result in a relapse.

A relapse is always possible if the addict has not learned alternate coping mechanisms as part of his or her recovery. The skills are not and cannot be achieved in seven to ten days of detox. In my years of nursing the addicted and working with those in recovery, my clients have often told me about feelings or triggers relating to the past. These people, in the recovery process or stabilized as recovered, were using coping techniques they learned in recovery. Their prognosis is more favourable if they voice the trigger experience rather than acting on it.

In the old days we had the Narcotic Addiction Foundation (N.A.F.). It was initially located at Broadway and Cypress and in the latter years at 307 West Broadway, not too far from the Vancouver General Hospital. Addicts made daily visits there for urine testing for drug abuse while on methadone prescribed by doctors on staff, and received counselling and referrals for detox and recovery. Strict guidelines outlined what behaviours constituted program abuse and what the consequences were. Unfortunately N.A.F.'s funding was terminated in the early 1970s by the provincial government of the time.

One addict succeeding in recovery is motivation for others. Ex-addicts should have respect and recognition in our society, and especially in the school system. I may walk the walk and talk the talk, but the addict in recovery actually stepped in it, cleaned his shoes and kept walking. He got his shit together and picked it up. Now this is a win–win situation that can benefit everyone. These resourceful people are the best ones to help others caught up in the downward spiral of addiction.

A man who recovered with help from the N.A.F. program later dedicated his life to addressing addiction and youth issues because of his own addiction and recovery. Although the service was at first focused on youth, John Turvey didn't pull services once his clients reached the age of majority. No, he expanded them to encompass the change and ended by aggressively addressing all issues relating to Vancouver's Downtown Eastside.

I knew him for forty years, both in good times and bad. I first met him while I was employed at the N.A.F. and thirty years later I was an employee under his direction, on the Downtown Eastside Health Outreach Van through D.E.Y.A.S.

All regular employees of D.E.Y.A.S. were addicts in recovery for two years or more. Often they started out by sweeping, cleaning and emptying wastebaskets in the office, but they were proud to have John Turvey hire them and even prouder to wear a D.E.Y.A.S. t-shirt.

John Turvey gave everything to develop and build the Downtown Eastside Youth Activities Services Society. He was honoured provincially with the Lieutenant Governor's Award for his dedication and service and received the Order of Canada posthumously in 2006. His memory lived on in D.E.Y.A.S., a monument to the fact that he never forgot his roots or his pledge to strive for action and resolution.

Twenty-two:
The Missing Women

One night, on our last run through the Stroll, I saw a vehicle moving along Railway Street about a block ahead of us. It was very dark but I mentioned, "What's with that truck? It looks like a garbage bag hanging out the passenger window." We saw a flash of white from the "bag" as it passed under a streetlight and I said, "I think it's a girl!"

My driver put his foot on the gas and literally raced at the truck, honking the horn. The person or people in the truck cab let the "bag" fall and roll to the curb, while the vehicle took off like a shot. We could not see the plate number or describe it as anything other than an older truck. Besides, there was an injured girl who required our attention!

She was hysterical. She was crying so hard that she just hugged me at first. After getting her into the Van, I began checking her injuries. She had had a clump of her dark hair pulled out; her scalp was bleeding slightly; there was road rash on her knees, ankles and toes and a small swelling on the left side of her face. While I was cleaning her up and applying dressings, I told her that we needed to call the police. She began screaming and crying all over again, saying, "No, no, please, no, Bonnie!"

We drove away from the area, parked and continued talking to the girl, trying to get information about the person or people involved. She refused any information other than, "He wanted a date and I didn't want to go."

I said to her, "Did you know the guy?"

She looked at me and said, "*No!*"

I told her, "You know you can trust me. Please tell us; we go back so many years, girl!" She continued to refuse any information but she did say, "I'd be dead."

We documented the information that we were able to see and treat for the D.E.Y.A.S. bad date sheet. We were a confidential service—we could not intervene in any other way if the client was rational and refused. The girl could have refused any treatment, could have refused to talk to us or even walked away. Our hands were tied unless we happened upon an assault taking place right in front of our eyes while driving the van—then we immediately called the police. We had to assure our own safety first or we couldn't help at all.

During the time I worked on the Health Van, the police and other authorities received many reports of women missing from the Downtown Eastside—for years in some cases. Agencies involved with these women on a regular basis submitted these reports. The "Missing Women" were known and cared for by many services in the Downtown Eastside.

For instance, we on the Health Outreach Van and Needle Exchange knew these girls were not around because we also worked a good portion of their "working hours." As time went on we realized the problem was not going away, it was getting worse. Where were these women?

"What happened to her? Have you seen… ?" It was agonizing for everyone: the clients and all of us who had known these girls for many years. Welfare cheques had not been collected, bank accounts had no activity, rooms still contained their untouched belongings. Anxiety over the ever-increasing list of missing women continued without any active investigation for over eight years. Where were they? Did anyone care?

How many lives might have been saved if the many rumours and suspicions had been investigated? We all had bits and pieces of information that could have been investigated and ruled out.

D.E.Y.A.S. and the W.I.S.H. Society, in particular, had concerns about specific people, male and female, who we believed had information or were persons of interest. Both programs used gut feelings based on the word on the street and, in a couple of cases, on trauma injuries we'd seen. But without proof it was still just hearsay or thirdhand. W.I.S.H. kept a close watch on certain women acting in a suspicious way toward others who were vulnerable to any suggestion of a "free party."

Families of the missing were also worried about their daughters, sisters and friends. Professional contacts had not seen or heard from many of them either. These women were hard core and addicted but most never forgot their families. Phone calls, letters and cards kept them connected. I often received calls on the Health Van from a mom or other family member, asking us to check on a girl. When we did sometimes we had some good stuff to tell the family, or we stood by until the girl actually made the call. The requests grew as the list grew but the good stuff was not there to tell them.

Over a period of eight years the list grew to more than sixty-five prostitutes who had worked in the Downtown Eastside and who were unaccounted for. The list continued to grow. It was certainly my opinion and that of others that the Vancouver police did not place a priority on investigating this. Were these disposable women: addicts and others not worth worrying about?

Me and Constable Dickson at the fundraising run for W.I.S.H., 2005

Constable Dave Dickson worked the Stroll area. He spoke along with me at W.I.S.H. information sessions. He was one officer who was trusted by the girls, but one man can't do everything!

The city did little to assist the police—it did not provide funds to hire more police officers. What a toll it took on society and on the police chief. The police were overworked; how could progress be made toward making the streets safer without having the manpower to do the job?

It took many years and public outcry to finally initiate a comprehensive, cooperative team to investigate this serious issue. A task force of ten officers from various jurisdictions was finally assigned to the case of the "Missing Women" at that time. While most of the members were R.C.M.P. and the R.C.M.P. coordinated the investigation, the task force was housed at V.P.D. headquarters. It worked across all municipal jurisdictions.

The task force's focus was on determining who the women were and when they were last seen by various people working in the D.T.E.S. Manny and I were asked to go to the force's office in 2001 where we found a large poster made up of pictures of sixty or more missing women. There were no identifying names or information beneath the pictures. We were asked to identify as many of the women as possible by name. We explained to the team present that some of the names we knew were actual true names while we knew others by street names. In some cases we knew both.

It was heartwrenching to look at each picture. We were successful in fully identifying about forty women although we knew 90 percent of the group by face alone.

The very first picture on the poster was Sereena Abotsway. She was also known as Riviera Abotsway. I choked up upon looking at this girl's picture. She had been like a daughter to me and had visited me for a chat every shift that I worked. Sereena was at the W.I.S.H. Society most evenings for supper. She was active with her input and involvement on a committee that helped establish rules for the W.I.S.H. facility at the First United Church, on Gore Street near East Hastings.

I knew Sereena for about fifteen years—behind jail bars and on the street. Her history was dysfunctional, sad and lonely. In her youth she was a pretty girl of First Nations heritage raised by foster parents in Pitt Meadows. She had very strong feelings for her foster parents and maintained a connection "only when I'm straight." I saw her several times at Coquitlam Centre Mall when she was visiting her foster family.

One time I was there with my daughter and heard a loud yell, "Mom!" The cry almost echoed in the large mall and a girl in pink spandex came running to me. I gave her a hug while my teenaged daughter stood back with a confused look on her face, wondering, "Who is this girl?!" That was Sereena, my Riviera Abotsway!

A few years later, Sereena sustained serious scarring to her face when she was attacked with a broken bottle. It isn't clear to me whether the attacker was a bad date, a pimp or another working girl. The women were very territorial about their working areas and strongly discouraged trespassing by others. Sereena no longer had an unblemished, attractive appearance. She had deep scars from the trauma that extended from her left eye area down to her mouth.

I told the task force about the last time I'd seen Sereena. They asked me what made it stand out so solidly in my memory. I explained that the Health Van had a regular stop at 10:00 PM at "Crosswalk," on Hastings near Cambie Street and Victory Square. The Salvation Army staffed a drop-in there during the day, and when the drop-in closed at 10 PM they replaced the tables and chairs with mats on the floor for homeless men and women who needed a safe place to sleep. There was always a long line-up of men and several women waiting for Crosswalk to open its doors for the night. The space was limited so many people booked a spot earlier in the evening and returned at 10. Any spaces left were given to people in line, in order. Women slept in a back room while men slept in the larger storefront area.

It was a late summer evening in 2001 when we pulled up to Crosswalk. There were the usual requests for Tylenol, lozenges, bandaids and vitamins. Sereena was off to one side of the line-up calling, "Hi, Mom; can I talk to you when you have time?"

She came to sit inside after the requests were finished. I immediately exclaimed, "Wow, you sure are all dressed up and looking good!" She was wearing black heels, fishnet stockings, a short red faux-leather skirt and a black camisole covered by a sheer black, silky long-sleeved blouse. Her dark hair was clean and brushed fashionably, and her face made up carefully with bright-red lipstick.

Sereena excitedly said, "I'm going to a party and they are picking me up at Victory Square around 11:00 PM." She went back to the Square following our visit and and hugs from Manny and me. Both of us told her to be careful and that we'd see her tomorrow...

I told the police about the statistical comment sheets we kept for each shift that gave a first name and a brief description of the reason why every person visited the Health Van. I looked through our contact sheets, located the documentation of Sereena's visit to the Van and the details of the visit. I forwarded a copy to the investigating team.

We never saw Sereena Riviera Abotsway after that evening. I really missed seeing her. Manny just had a gut feeling that something bad had happened. One officer said that we may have been the last people to see her alive. Sereena Riviera Abotsway and what she was wearing that night is in my memory to this very day.

A coloured poster with pictures of the women, their identification details and date last seen was finally put together by the police in 2001. A very long investigation resulted in the arrest of Robert "Willie" Pickton for the murders of the missing women in 2002. I had no interest in attending the preliminary hearings in Port Coquitlam Provincial Court or the subsequent lengthy trial in Supreme Court. I did not want to listen to the gory details and I certainly did not want to look at Pickton.

Twenty-three:
Zapped in Seconds

I'd known John Turvey for forty years, from his youth in heroin addiction to adulthood in recovery. He was on my caseload at the Narcotic Addiction Foundation during his tough years and later I lost track of him during my own family years. I was amazed and thrilled to see what he did in 1980—he established the office of D.E.Y.A.S. at 223 Main Street while my worksite was Vancouver Provincial Court at 222 Main.

John and I renewed our friendship over the twenty-eight years I was at the courthouse and then I joined D.E.Y.A.S. Together we continued planning and expanding the Health Outreach Clinic Van program in 1999.

In the summer of 2003, Manny and I scheduled our annual vacation. We were looking forward to a well-deserved rest away from D.E.Y.A.S. Sad to say, but D.E.Y.A.S. had become an unhappy place to work in the spring of 2003. John Turvey was working limited hours due to poor health and many things began to change in his absence.

The D.E.Y.A.S. office moved to a Gastown location (in Blood Alley) following John's medically-based retirement. In retrospect it was not a good move—we were too far away from the action on Main. In fact, since Gastown was a tourist area, D.T.E.S. residents were often subject to "no go" orders and complaints by local businesses, and many addicts found it too far to walk from their connections. Many who came were advised to "move along" so they did not affect visitors' image of the city!

The street nurses who had always been upstairs on Main Street were relocated to Pender Street. I don't think that was a good idea, either. The split location made it harder to work cooperatively with them and clients could no longer access both services in one convenient location.

At the same time, long-time counsellor Dede Nelson left D.E.Y.A.S. to pursue her career in a different locale. A lot of heart went with her; she was so trusted by staff and more important, by her long list of ongoing clients. We sorely missed her dedication, although what she probably missed the most were Manny's shoulder massages!

Also that spring, numerous disgruntled employees had begun to discuss unionizing. D.E.Y.A.S. was one of the only societies in the D.T.E.S. that was not unionized. The talking ended in voting and the D.E.Y.A.S. employees became members of the Health Employees' Union (H.E U.).

Manny and I didn't want to unionize initially. We didn't see the need for it, and we hoped John Turvey would be well enough to come back at some point. We were happy with John at the helm. But it became obvious that he would not return, and we knew we could not avoid it. Manny became an H.E.U. member.

As D.E.Y.A.S's only full-time nurse, it made sense for me to become a member of the British Columbia Nurses' Union (B.C.N.U.). The relief nurses were already members of B.C.N.U. at their primary place of employment. There was no conflict if they worked shifts at a non-unionized service.

B.C.N.U. requested that I vote to join (as the only nurse affected by the vote) and complete the union membership form. I voted and signed the membership with Manny and the H.E.U. rep as witnesses, and gave the papers to the B.C.N.U.'s union rep, Moe. But not long after, the D.E.Y.A.S. executive claimed I was management and therefore ineligible for union membership. The end of the story would not be told until months later, after the B.C.N.U. took the issue to arbitration to argue my case.

In the meantime, it had been a busy shift on the Van and at the office on July 31, 2003, our last shift before our holidays. Manny was busy preparing information for the relief Health Van drivers

Manny and me in July 2003.

and I was ordering enough supplies to cover the weeks that the relief nurses would be covering for me. I had a bit of a headache while driving home, and chalked it up to being tired. I paid it no heed.

On August 1, 2003, I suffered a ruptured brain aneurysm to the left optic artery. I underwent brain surgery at Royal Columbian Hospital in New Westminster the same day. My whole life changed in a matter of seconds, only to be complicated further by unexpected open-heart surgery to repair two heart valves. I was a miracle survivor in the eyes of many, but in my own eyes I suddenly became someone who needed help, not one who helped.

B.C.N.U. won the arbitration battle for me in 2004, with the help and hard work of the relief nurses, who appeared on my behalf against the D.E.Y.A.S. claim. I could not speak for myself.

I went through a period of anxiety and depression that spanned about a year. I had to train my damaged brain to access my recent memories, render appropriate verbal responses and deal with basic physical disabilities related to my brain and heart trauma. Simple things like swallowing food, speaking without stuttering and keeping my balance were challenges for me. I lost in many other ways, including financially and in self-worth and self-esteem.

Pre-2003 memories were clear in my mind but I had to accept the fact that I was not the person that I used to be. I had to begin to get on with my life. My motivation to make a change in my attitude was twofold: learning that I was going to be a grandma and looking at myself in the mirror and saying, "You have always been a tough old broad. Get on with it—write that book your mom always said you should write!" In spring 2005, I did just that and now you are reading it!

Twenty-four:
Epilogue

My interest in the D.T.E.S. and D.E.Y.A.S. did not change after my enforced disability retirement in 2003. I shared words at a candlelight memorial at Pigeon Square for John Turvey, who passed away October 11, 2006 from his illness. Many clients attended along with D.E.Y.A.S. staff members. Sweet Janet saw me there, rushed home and baked a cheese bannock for her "Mom." When she returned to give it to me, it was still hot.

Janet and me, 2002

It was televised on the local news and covered in the newspapers, showing the utmost respect for a man who devoted his life to the have-not citizens of our city. John Turvey received the Lieutenant Governor's Award for his innovative services in B.C. He was awarded the Order of Canada posthumously as well.

I also kept in touch with the families and friends of the missing women. The court decided that the murder charges against Robert "Willie" Pickton would be heard and judged in divided groups due to the number of victims and the amount of evidence. In December, 2007 I went to New Westminster Supreme Court during the sequestering of the trial jury. My wish was to be there behind the one-way glass in the Family Room on the second floor of the courtroom, to see and hear the jury's decision on the first six murders. The jury reached its decision after nine days: guilty of second-degree murder. On December 11, 2007, Robert Pickton was sentenced to a twenty-five years for each of the six murders, to be served concurrently.

There were cheers and tears from family and friends on hearing the decision of the jury. Right after sentencing, families and close friends formed a candle circle outside the courthouse. Elaine Allan, a long-time advocate for the missing women and former staff member of the W.I.S.H. Society, was asked to read the names and speak on behalf of the friends and families. She announced the names of all the missing women and a small candle was lit for each, from tapers carried by chosen participants and family.

It was a very moving memorial. I had a lump in my throat when I was asked by the families to hold a taper and join the circle. The ceremonial experience was deeply heartfelt.

At the end of the tribute, Elaine announced, "There is one person especially that the families wish to thank for her determined effort on behalf of their loved ones, and that is Bonnie Fournier, the nurse on the former D.E.Y.A.S. Health Outreach Van." I burst into tears on hearing those words: tears for the girls, tears for the families and tears for myself.

Many things changed for D.E.Y.A.S. during that time. The Youth Detox Centre was denied funding in 2004, along with the youth street workers on the Youth Car.

In the spring of 2005 D.E.Y.A.S. retired the Health Van due to lack of funding, and staffing problems—the service had difficulty finding someone who could work well with Manny while handling the necessary nursing. The van and the program went into the crushed metal pile. There has been no clinic van service since then. The loss is unspeakable for those who worked and those in need.

Manny moved over to the Rig Van, which continued its work with addicts in the D.T.E.S. The D.E.Y.A.S. office moved from Blood Alley to a temporary office on Main Street off Pender in 2005 and moved again in 2006 to a storefront on East Broadway.

The Rig Van continued to provide full exchange services and referrals under the supervision of Manny Cu. Other dedicated employees struggled to maintain and restore full D.E.Y.A.S. services to the D.T.E.S.

In 2008, I was asked if I would stand for election to the D.E.Y.A.S. board of directors. I agreed and was elected along with another person. The previous board monitored the election process and then resigned. The only former board member who remained was Paul Taylor from Carnegie Centre; a long-time advocate and resident of the D.T.E.S. Three other people joined the board with us: a youth in recovery and two others from the community. I was elected temporary president until the annual general meeting in the spring of 2009.

The new board met with funding bodies in the D.T.E.S. and worked collaboratively with other services such as W.I.S.H., which was also being denied funding for their Mobile Access Program (M.A.P.). While not as comprehensive as what D.E.Y.A.S. provided, their service was still viable. Without a nurse they referred and called E.H.S. *prn*. M.A.P. was the only multipurpose service left providing harm reduction to D.T.E.S. residents in the night hours. At D.E.Y.A.S. we did our best to beat the bushes but the funding just wasn't there for what the Ministry of Health deemed "duplication of existing services," while trying to deny funding to that existing service as well.

In summer 2009, D.E.Y.A.S. closed the doors to its East Broadway office. Sadly, it was the end of an era. The needle exchange program, however, continued operation out of the RainCity Housing Facility (formerly Triage) with funding from the Vancouver Coastal Health Authority. It was good judgment by Vancouver Coastal Health to recognize Manny Cu's ability, expertise and dedication as the best man for the job. I am delighted that the exchange service has continued under his management.

W.I.S.H. successfully obtained funding on appeal for the M.A.P. Van, and it is back on the road. I will continue my interest in the D.T.E.S. although I am unable to visit as often as I would like. I make my voice heard by supporting Carnegie Centre Housing Coalition, and I take my hat off to Wendy Pedersen and others who keep the fires burning, forcing governments to provide housing and services to Vancouver's homeless population.

Never forget that the greatest of achievements were at first and for a time just dreams. The dreams are over; it is time to face reality and foster positive achievements in a society set aside and sorely ignored for many years.

Twenty-five:
Put Humpty Dumpty Together Again

The primary needs of all human beings are air, food, water, housing, love and self-appreciation. All of these are necessary for us to be able to challenge and resolve the difficulties we face during our lifetimes. Primary concerns are technology and lifestyle changes (positively or negatively) at any level of society. The drugs, violence and offences against others that I witnessed over so many years were, in most cases, only symptoms of a primary problem. They were the secondary results of not meeting one or more primary human needs. I call this the Humpty Dumpty consequence.

Societal adjustments that allow us to continue providing help to people in need have been disappearing with each passing decade. We are seeing the subtle demise of a system of values that provided a firm foundation for family life, caring and involvement in our society for hundreds of years.

I believe that education and intervention can work to reverse this trend if credible ideas come from aware, dedicated, on-the-spot professionals. Many people who ask for their help and advice are desperate and devastated and not punching a timeclock.

You will find the knowledge at the grass roots level—listen and ask for direction toward resolution. Healing cannot start if our government, and society in general, lack or ignore the grass roots facts.

Listen with the goal of moving forward. Acknowledge, humbly, that ignorance is not bliss. The misery is visible and committed agencies and services are already there. We have all the evidence of need but scattered funding is a waste. We must have funding that ensures continuity of intervention to make a difference that will be reflected throughout modern society and positively motivated into honest and committed action.

Agencies must also work together to fill cracks and holes in coordinated services and intervention. Need continues after agency hours and is aggravated further when continuity of care is not followed up on weekends or stat holidays.

Trust and communication between agencies and compromised citizens allow them to connect and interact cooperatively, which is actually more cost-effective than over-funding services independently. A continuum of care from intervention to assessment, detox, treatment and ultimately recovery must be a common goal.

Shuffling the deck or moving money from one pocket to another does not work but desire and motivation to complete the circle will. Strive toward resolution, not enabling.

You cannot make a silk purse out of a sow's ear, to coin a phrase, but dedicated employees have always provided the best services possible with the funding they get each budget year. The statistics and expertise are free for the asking—no tax dollars need to be spent to "strike a committee to study the problem." The real committee has been there all along to inform, react, educate, intervene and plead for action and funding. We who have worked in the area for many years *are* the committee. We have the answers to the questions. Just ask us, walk with us, ride with us and see for yourself.

I am appalled by ignorance and comments like, "They made the choice to live that life. I'm not interested in listening or providing..." Hey, big spender, open your eyes and look in your own backyard, maybe in your own family. It is there but you look the other way, saying that it's not your problem. Would you walk past a drowning man because after all, it was his decision to go on the boat ride without knowing how to swim? It was his choice and it's not your problem? With that said, put your feet up and enjoy a martini or two. That's your choice.

Nobody is asking you to fix something that ain't broke. We are asking you for your support to fix something that is broken. It is beyond the could-have, would-have and should-have stages.

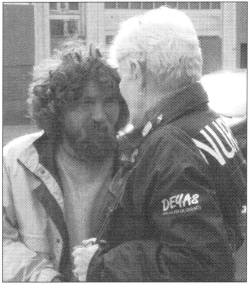

My book speaks to societal problems that exist in any civilized city worldwide. I nursed thirty-three years in this anti-social environment. Emotional, psychological and physical devastation was my teacher.

The drugs we are seeing on the street today are quickly produced in large amounts and provide big bucks for the producer. Ingredients are readily obtainable and sales are strong at all levels of society. The result is dysfunction and the deterioration of treasured and respected societal mores.

There is no so-called "druggie corner" in our cities anymore; drugs are available everywhere, including Kerrisdale, Point Grey, English Bay and out at the University. Manny and I were once called to identify a body in St. Paul's hospital morgue. It was a beautiful girl from a wonderful upper class family, who had died of an overdose in the Hazelwood Hotel on East Hastings. We waited at St. Paul's for her parents after we'd confirmed who it was. Manny and I knew the girl's mom well, because she had been downtown many times looking for her beloved daughter. So very sad for everyone!

The problem is no longer epidemic but endemic. As I've said before, the mean age of youth experimenting with crystal meth, crack cocaine and Ecstasy is twelve years, with little gender distinction. Teachers are noticing marked changes in attendance, attitude, peer association and motivation. Parents are embarrassed and feel like failures. They are often in denial until the fabric of the family is seriously threatened. Don't forget to lock up your computer monitor cleaning fluid, because they're huffing it!

The "corner" is no longer the place where drugs are. Now it is where the pain and misery of the addict, the marginalized, the dually-diagnosed and the poverty-stricken are visible to people on transit or in cars. But seeing them isn't enough. People avoid "going through there" instead of thinking about what they see and what they can do. The question is, what can individuals do if their government doesn't seem to care?

In many cases a token budget is allotted and then the governing political party takes a bow for carrying through on an election promise. But a band-aid application of miserly funding will not slow the deterioration of the Downtown Eastside. The term "homeless" is misunderstood by society and glossed over by our elected officials. Our own prime minister, Stephen Harper, made media statements recently that used the word "junkies" in reference to Downtown Eastside residents.

Look in the mirror, politicians at all levels of government. The image reflected is one of gross negligence toward those interpreted as disposable people. Lumping all Downtown Eastsiders into the "junkie" category is indicative of the same attitude that led to irresponsible delays in acting on the long list of women missing from the area.

Meanwhile political "junkies" band-aid over the issues of the Downtown Eastside, misinforming and placating the people who elected them and trusted their mandate. In 2008 a $100 monetary "fix" was mailed to every citizen in the province of British Columbia by the finance minister as a "climate action dividend"—even to addicts and prisoners!

Hmmm, no buzz, no high, not even pain relief for the Downtown Eastside. Think about the total dollars sent out and how much harm reduction we could have received for that amount.

Members of our provincial government got a substantial increase in salary a while ago, more than any collective agreement settlement for hardworking union members, those on approved long-term disability, minimum wage or worthy welfare recipients. It is time to stop rewarding negative behaviour by our governments. We are paying for their gas and they are giving us flatus in return. Trust me on this—I am a retired nurse and no longer a mouth breather.

About the Author

Bonnie Fournier was born in Powell River, B.C. in 1944. She graduated as a registered psychiatric nurse (R.P.N.) in 1966 following three years of hospital training at the Essondale (later Riverview) Hospital in Coquitlam. She specialized in forensic and addictions nursing after 1968. She is now retired and lives in Coquitlam, B.C. She is the proud grandmother of three grandsons.

Me with the Health Van across from the courthouse, 2003